TWO
STITCHES

TWO
STITCHES

Jewelry Projects in Peyote & Right Angle Weave

RACHEL NELSON-SMITH

LARK
New York

LARK
New York

An Imprint of Sterling Publishing
1166 Avenue of the Americas
New York, NY 10036

Text and illustrations © 2015 by Rachel Nelson-Smith
Photography © 2015 by Lark Crafts

ISBN 978-1-4547-0873-5

Distributed in Canada by Sterling Publishing
c/o Canadian Manda Group, 664 Annette Street
Toronto, Ontario, Canada M6S 2C8
Distributed in the United Kingdom by GMC Distribution Services
Castle Place, 166 High Street, Lewes, East Sussex, England BN7 1XU
Distributed in Australia by Capricorn Link (Australia) Pty. Ltd.
P.O. Box 704, Windsor, NSW 2756, Australia

For information about custom editions, special sales, and premium and
corporate purchases, please contact Sterling Special Sales at 800-805-5489
or specialsales@sterlingpublishing.com.

Manufactured in China

10 9 8 7 6 5 4 3 2 1

larkcrafts.com

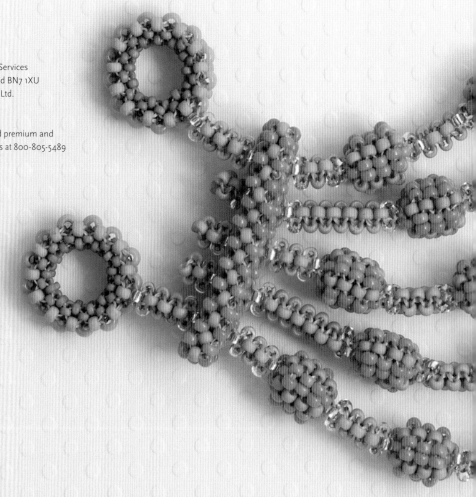

Contents

Introduction

Bead shows are incredibly delightful events. My intent is to bring that bead bliss into your home with projects designed as though they were offered as workshops at national bead events. While several projects are on a smaller scale, the majority are substantial and could be described as ginormous.

As many beaders continue to discover, right angle weave and peyote stitch work well together, producing unlimited design possibilities. In these pages, the beadweaving projects are set forth as examples and jumping-off points. Each project allows for your own explorations into the stitch combination.

The peyote bead sprinkled throughout the projects initially occurred in the first Mother's Meditation Necklace I made and wore during my pregnancy. I meditated on the 40 beads representing 40 weeks of gestation, and as my fingers rose and fell over the beads, the projects came to me one by one—always watchful for the seamless connection between the two stitches.

As for the colors, the brightness and verve for life can be explained by the joy I've experienced as a new mother. A fondness for the combinations of olivine and fuchsia, red and fuchsia, and turquoise with gold or bronze led me to design the projects primarily in these colors.

The 11° round seed bead is a ubiquitous material, easy to find, readily available, and versatile. It is the primary material not only for the lengths and structures of the projects, but also for the closures and focal pieces.

I hope you enjoy these projects, whether you execute them to the letter or incorporate their ideas into your own bead practice.

Fundamentals

Everything starts somewhere, and when it comes to these projects, the next few pages of fundamental information and techniques are where it's at. Referring to this information and taking the basic bead lessons to heart will help your understanding and result in sound beadwork.

THE NITTY-GRITTY

The beginning is a very good place to start. Get to the crux of the favored stitches—right angle weave and tubular peyote stitch—and how they interweave. Mind all the goodness of these opening pages, and get set on a path of beady righteousness. You'll learn heaps of techniques, and your work will persist and even be passed on to the next generation—if you're into that sort of thing.

DOUBLE-STITCH EVERYTHING: IT'S THAT IMPORTANT

Well, almost everything. Always double-stitch if you want your work to last. So much time is spent to create a beadwoven piece that you don't want a weak threaded area to break the first time it is worn. Then, the piece languishes in disrepair and neglect at the back of some dark drawer. You know of what I speak!

You spend an immense about of time to complete a beadweaving project, so why not make sure it will last? Many factors contribute to the longevity of beadwork, including some that are beyond our control—say, how much a bracelet is worn by your sister or if she ill-advisedly washes dishes while wearing it. The main factor we can control is beadwork strength. This is why all the beadwork here is double-stitched. The difference double-stitching makes is evinced in these two samples—note the increased body of the doubled-stitched sample on the left.

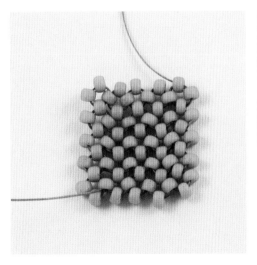 

So, yes. Double-stitching will detract from your other leisure activities, like pulling garden weeds, but believe me, it will pay off in the end. Even your diva dish-doing sister will have handmade beadwork that will last.

MOUNT FOR ADVENTURE

Consider yourself a crafter of fine things. Ask your fine crafting self if you would use a cheap clasp that is prone to breaking. Ask your inner purveyor of all things quality if a cheap thread will do. With gusto say yes to materials and beads from Germany, or Japan, or even the United States! Otherwise, any effort you make will more likely end up going down the drain when the cheap clasp breaks or the plastic thread snaps! When you craft fine works with skill, employ that skill in the assembly and in the selection of materials and tools.

MATERIAL SELECTION

Items used in the body of the work are included here. Items can run out, so consider gathering more than you need—besides, you can call it building your inventory! All seed beads used here are Japanese and selected for their beautiful color and hole size. All crystal beads and crystal stones are selected for their consistency and exceptional sparkle. (Crystal stones are solid crystal and have no hole.) Threads are selected for exceptional color and appropriate thickness—as nearly all this beadwork is double-stitched, a considerable amount of thread is used. Select quality findings to ensure a strong finish to your work, and attach them in a way they can easily be replaced in case of malfunction.

Japanese seed beads are colorful and consistent.

Crystal beads add a lot or a little sparkle. The bicone shape is my favorite.

Crystal stones make for eye-catching centerpieces.

Thread comes in many colors to match every beadweaving project.

Navigating My Illustrations

Though the word *string* is used, each bead is counted as being added with a single stitch, and stitch counts include every pass made through each individual bead.

Active stitch paths are red, blue, green, black, gold, lavender, rose, aqua, brown, or chartreuse. They appear in this order when multiple steps are shown—unless a different color path is needed for clarity. Inactive stitch paths are gray.

Thread paths are shown as dashed when passing through the top layer of beads. Thread paths are not shown when passing through the back layers of beads.

Red, green, and blue dots are used to indicate key beads in a project. The beads are not actually dotted, nor do they require dots to be drawn upon them.

A white-filled red circle indicates stitch path origination point.

A color-filled dot indicates a knot.

Arrows indicate stitch path direction.

Solid lines indicate exposed thread between beads.

Beads are illustrated with gaps between them for clarity. Use appropriate thread tension to avoid gaps in your beadwork.

"Just added" refers to the beads most recently added, and "last added" refers to the bead or beads added before those just added.

Multistrand clasps are used to finish the ends of some projects.

Closed jump rings make a great transition point from beadwork to finding loops.

Use open jump rings to connect soldered jump rings to finding loops. They have many uses.

WORKSPACE SETUP

Make a comfortable place to work. Give yourself a chair that supports you and a work surface at a comfortable height. Put a glass of water at your side—a watercooler is even better. When you are comfortable, you can focus and get some good work done. Naturally, it is helpful to have a bathroom nearby.

Beadweaving Kit

Make a comfortable place to work. Give yourself a chair that supports you, and a work surface at a comfortable height. These are items to have on hand when doing beadwork at home.

Work on the inside face of medium-weight leather—and draw on it when a break is needed.

These scissors provide a close cut in a compact package.

#12 needles are the key to creating these beadwork projects. Though they bend and break, needles are the workhorses of off-loom beadweaving.

Keep needles safe in a beloved beaded needle case. The wood case shown was my grandmother's, but you can find one at your local bead shop.

#15 needles are for tricky, tiny spots. I rarely use them, but when you need them, you really need them.

Pinch a needle with a thick rubber band to push it through a thread-stuffed bead hole—without breaking the bead, of course.

Keep a bead awl on hand for breaking bad beads. The Tulip awl is especially fine.

A full-spectrum light keeps things bright.

Chain-nose pliers are used for opening and closing jump rings and getting a good grip on a needle. I prefer German-made pliers for reliability, and the metal grips needles better than lesser-made pliers.

THE STITCHES

With so many stitches, how do we choose just two? Using right angle weave and peyote stitch together is like discovering the compatibility of peanut butter and jelly, or popcorn and movies—they are simply and wonderfully complementary. Since making the first Ootheca Cuff in 2005, I have been obsessed with the combination. You may dig into these projects because they are visually appealing, but I hope you can find the rhythm that exists within this stitch combination.

The form of each stitch is very basic. We make it complicated by repeating the stitches and bending them to our will.

Right Angle Weave

Flexible and fabric-like, this stitch can be a beader's bane or boon. It is no fancy stitch, and there's nothing new about it. This stitch is double-stitched in every instance it is used. With a single thread pass, the beadwork is wimpy and prone to broken threads—matte seed beads, crystals, and metal beads are notorious for this. With a reinforced stitch, the resulting beadwork is considerably more toothy and durable.

In the basic form of right angle weave, flat is where it is at. All right angle weave begins in this form and then is manipulated into various shapes. As simple as it is, the way I work right angle weave may come as a surprise. It requires a little more time and is worth it in the end. Rather than adding a unit and moving to add the following unit, each unit is reinforced before moving on. Unless specified otherwise, all pieces calling for right angle weave employ this approach.

This stitch comes in the flat form only, as any modification follows different principles. How to finish and add threads is included at the end of the section.

PRINCIPLE 1

Imagine a clock face—no, not your phone's digital clock, but a classic clock face, the one with twelve numbers on it and two sweeping hands. Actually, you don't have to imagine it; just look at the lovely illustration I drew for you. We know the time by locating the two sweeping hands. Which way do they sweep? That's right! They go clockwise. They do not actually go counterclockwise, but that is certainly a direction we will go—and one we are going to use quite a bit. See figure 1.

PRINCIPLE 2

Now, I'm going to ask you to think back to being a teenager—sorry! Remember geometry class? Recall the topic of angles? Which was the easiest angle to remember? The right angle. A 90° (right) angle is the angle that is formed at the intersection of two perpendicular lines, like a corner. We are not talking any obtuse 120° or acute 45° situations—that results in some very different beadwork. We are talking 90° only. See figure 2.

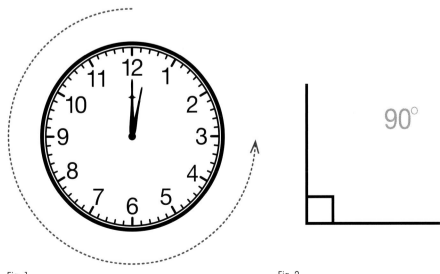

Fig. 1   Fig. 2

Lucky for us, the right angle was a concept recognized by whoever named right angle weave. Those smart people knew that every time they needed to made a subsequent stitch, the thread would travel at a right angle from the previous stitch.

Beginning in the bottom left, this swatch of five-row by five-row right angle weave is worked row by row to be five units wide and five units tall. Row 1 is the bottom row and row 5 is the top row. The gray arrows indicate the stitch direction. The gray numbers represent the number of stitches to complete before beginning a subsequent unit.

Note: The number of stitches to complete each unit does not include stringing beads or if you choose to pass through more than one bead in a single stitch.

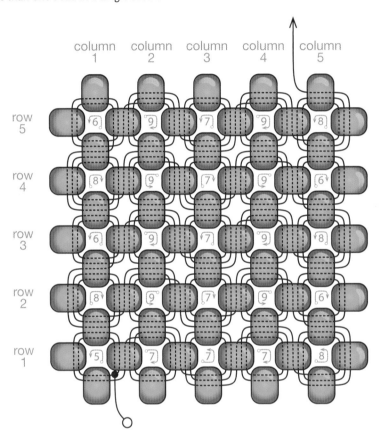

Fig. 3

Read the illustration from the bottom left to the bottom right for row 1. Read row 2 right to left, row 3 left to right, row 4 right to left, and row 5 left to right.

ROW 1, FIRST UNIT

String four beads, tie a knot, and work counterclockwise to pass through the first bead just added, the second bead just added, the third bead just added, the fourth bead just added, and the first bead just added. Five stitches complete the unit.

ROW 1, SECOND UNIT

String three beads and, working clockwise, stitch through the bead from the previous unit last stitched through, the first bead just added, the second bead just added, the third bead just added, the bead from the previous unit last stitched through, the first bead just added, and the second bead just added. Seven stitches complete the unit.

ROW 1, THIRD UNIT

String three beads and, working counterclockwise, stitch through the bead from the previous unit last stitched through, the first bead just added, the second bead just added, the third bead just added, the bead from the previous unit last stitched through, the first bead just added, and the second bead just added. Seven stitches complete the unit.

ROW 1, FOURTH UNIT

String three beads and, working clockwise, stitch through the bead from the previous unit last stitched through, the first bead just added, the second bead just added, the third bead just added, the bead from the previous unit last stitched through, the first bead just added, and the second bead just added. Seven stitches complete the unit.

ROW 1, FIFTH UNIT

String three beads and, working counterclockwise, stitch through bead from the previous unit last stitched through, the first bead just added, the second bead just added, the third bead just added, the bead from the previous unit last stitched through, the first bead just added, the second bead just added, and the third bead just added. Eight stitches complete the unit.

ROW 2, FIRST UNIT

String three beads and, working clockwise, stitch through the bead from the previous unit last stitched through, the first bead just added, the second bead just added, the third bead just added, the bead from the previous unit last stitched through (top bead of row 1/column 5), and the first bead just added. Six stitches complete the unit.

ROW 2, SECOND UNIT

String two beads and, working counterclockwise, stitch through the top bead of row 1/column 4, the bead from the previous unit last stitched through, the first bead just added, the second bead just added, the top bead of row 1/column 4, the bead from the previous unit last stitched through, the first bead just added, the second bead just added, and the top bead of row 1/column 3 (to the left). Nine stitches complete the unit.

ROW 2, THIRD UNIT

String two beads and, working clockwise, stitch through the bead from the previous unit last stitched through, the top bead of row 1/column 3, the first bead just added, the second bead just added, the bead from the previous unit last stitched through, the top bead of row 1/column 3, and the first bead just added. Seven stitches complete the unit.

ROW 2, FOURTH UNIT

String two beads and, working counterclockwise, stitch through the top row 1/column 2 bead, the bead from the previous unit last stitched through, the first bead just added, the second bead just added, the top bead of row 1/column 2, the bead from previous unit last stitched through, the first bead just added, the second bead just added, and the top bead of row 1/column 1 (to the left). Nine stitches complete the unit.

ROW 2, FIFTH UNIT

String two beads and, working clockwise, stitch through the bead from the previous unit last stitched through, the top bead of row 1/column 1, the first bead just added, the second bead just added, the bead from the previous unit last stitched through, the top bead of row 1/column 1, the first bead just added, and the second bead just added. Eight stitches complete the unit.

ROW 3, FIRST UNIT

String three beads and, working counterclockwise, stitch through the bead from the previous unit last stitched through, the first bead just added, the second bead just added, the third bead just added, the bead from the previous unit last stitched through (top bead of row 2/column 2), and the first bead just added. Six stitches complete the unit.

ROW 3, SECOND UNIT

String two beads and, working clockwise, stitch though the top row 2/column 2 bead, the bead from the previous unit last stitched through, the first bead just added, the second bead just added, the top bead of row 2/column 2, the bead from the previous unit last stitched through, the first bead just added, the second bead just added, and the top bead of row 2/column 3 to the right. Nine stitches complete the unit.

ROW 3, THIRD UNIT

String two beads and, working counterclockwise, stitch through the bead from the previous unit last stitched through, the top bead of row 2/column 3, the first bead just added, the second bead just added, the bead from the previous unit last stitched through, the top bead of row 2/column 3, and the first bead just added. Seven stitches complete the unit.

ROW 3, FOURTH UNIT

String two beads and, working clockwise, stitch through the top bead of row 2/column 4, the bead from the previous unit last stitched through, the first bead just added, the second bead just added, the top bead of row 2/column 4, the bead from the previous unit last stitched through, the first bead just added, the second bead just added, and the top bead of row 2/column 5 (to the right). Nine stitches complete the unit.

ROW 3, FIFTH UNIT

String two beads and, working counterclockwise, stitch through the bead from the previous unit last stitched through, the top bead of row 2/column 5, the first bead just added, the second bead just added, the bead from the previous unit last stitched through, the top bead of row 2/column 5, the first bead just added, and the second bead just added. Eight stitches complete the unit.

ROW 4, FIRST UNIT

String three beads and, working clockwise, stitch through the bead from the previous unit last stitched through (the top bead of row 3/column 5), the first bead just added, the second bead just added, the third bead just added, the bead from the previous unit last stitched through (the top bead of row 3/column 5), and the first bead just added. Six stitches complete the unit.

ROW 4, SECOND UNIT

String two beads and, working counterclockwise, stitch through the top bead of row 3/column 4, the bead from the previous unit last stitched through, the first bead just added, the second bead just added, the top bead of row 3/column 4, the bead from the previous unit last stitched through, the first bead just added, the second bead just added, and the top bead of row 3/column 3 (to the left). Nine stitches complete the unit.

ROW 4, THIRD UNIT

String two beads and, working clockwise, stitch through the leftmost bead of the previous unit, the top bead of row 3/column 3, the first bead just added, the second bead just added, the leftmost bead of the previous unit, the top bead of row 3/column 3, and the first bead just added. Seven stitches complete the unit.

ROW 4, FOURTH UNIT

String two beads and, working counterclockwise, stitch through the top bead of row 3/column 2, the bead from the previous unit last stitched through, the first bead just added, the second bead just added, the top bead of row 3/column 2, the bead from the previous unit last stitched through, the first bead just added, the second bead just added, and the top bead of row 3/column 1 (to the left). Nine stitches complete the unit.

ROW 4, FIFTH UNIT

String two beads and, working clockwise, stitch into the leftmost bead of the previous unit, the top bead of row 3/column 1, the first bead just added, the second bead just added, the leftmost bead of the previous unit, the top bead of row 3/column 1, the first bead just added, and the second bead just added. Eight stitches complete the unit.

ROW 5, FIRST UNIT

String three beads and, working counterclockwise, stitch into the bead from the previous unit last stitched through (the top bead of row 4/column 1), the first bead just added, the second bead just added, the third bead just added, the bead from the previous unit last stitched through (the top bead of row 4/column 1), and the first bead just added. Six stitches complete the unit.

ROW 5, SECOND UNIT

String two beads and, working clockwise, stitch into the top bead of row 4/column 2, the rightmost bead from the previous unit last stitched through, the first bead just added, the second bead just added, the top bead of row 4/column 2, the rightmost bead from the previous unit last stitched through, the first bead just added, the second bead just added, and the top bead of row 4/column 3, to the right. Nine stitches complete the unit.

ROW 5, THIRD UNIT

String two beads and, working counterclockwise, stitch into the rightmost bead from the previous unit last stitched through, the top bead of row 4/column 3, the first bead just added, the second bead just added, the rightmost bead from the previous unit last stitched through, the top bead of row 4/column 3, and the first bead just added. Seven stitches complete the unit.

ROW 5, FOURTH UNIT

String two beads and, working clockwise, stitch into the top bead of row 4/column 4, the rightmost bead from the previous unit last stitched through, the first bead just added, the second bead just added, the top bead of row 4/column 4, the rightmost bead from the previous unit last stitched through, the first bead just added, the second bead just added, and the top bead of row 4/column 5 (to the right). Nine stitches complete the unit.

ROW 5, FIFTH UNIT

String two beads and, working counterclockwise, stitch into the rightmost bead from the previous unit last stitched through, the top bead of row 4/column 5, the first bead just added, the second bead just added, the rightmost bead from the previous unit last stitched through, the top bead of row 4/column 5, the first bead just added, and the second bead just added. Eight stitches complete the unit.

PATTERNS

Find patterns within the illustration. The first unit and row are unique. The stitch patterns and number of beads will not be repeated again.

STITCH COUNT

The unit requiring the least number of stitches is the first unit. The units requiring the most stitches are the even-count units in each row—for example, units 2 and 4 are created with a whopping nine stitches. Note that the stitch count patterns on the left and right edges are complementary—except for the first unit.

DIRECTION

Each unit is created in either the clockwise or the counterclockwise direction. A unit created with clockwise stitches is always surrounded on all four sides by units created with counterclockwise stitches.

FINISHING AND ADDING THREAD

It is essential to know how to begin and end threads within these projects because not one of them can be completed with a single thread. Your working thread should be no more than 2 yards (1.8 m) long, or about fingertip to fingertip with your arms outstretched.

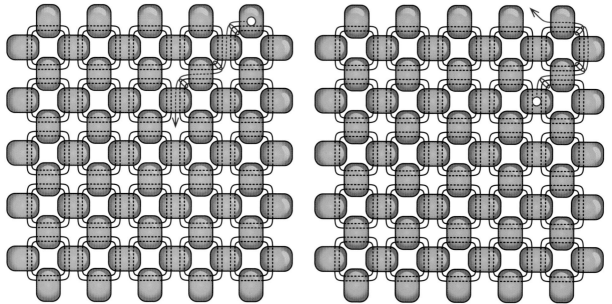

Fig. 4, finish a thread   Fig. 5, add a thread

Finish a thread when it is about 6 inches (15 cm) long. Beginning in the top right, stitch through the final bead, wind a half-hitch knot around the adjacent thread, stitch down through an adjacent bead, wind a half-hitch knot around the existing adjacent thread, stitch left through an adjacent bead, wind a half-hitch knot around the existing adjacent thread, stitch down through an adjacent bead, and cut the thread close to where it last exits. See figure 4.

To add a thread, cut a working length of thread and stitch through a bead four stitches away from where the beadwork will continue. Wind a half-hitch knot around the adjacent thread, stitch right through the adjacent bead, wind a half-hitch knot around the existing adjacent thread, stitch up through the adjacent bead, wind a half-hitch knot around the adjacent thread, stitch left through the adjacent bead, and continue the beadwork pattern. See figure 5.

RIGHT ANGLE WEAVE RING
This ring is made with 15° and 11° round seed beads and 3mm crystals in flat right angle shaped into a tube. Stitch three rows and close it with the fourth. The ring length (units long) varies to suit each project. Use it to complete the projects Lublinea Necklace, Vertann Necklace, B'Alexander Earrings, Quattuor Earrings, Bienenbaus Bracelet, Nacho Libre Bracelet, and Pop Bead Bracelet.

1. Work a strip of right angle weave three units wide with 11°s and 15°s in the first row, 15°s in the second (middle) row, and 15°s and 11°s in the third row. Make the strip the number of units specified in the project.

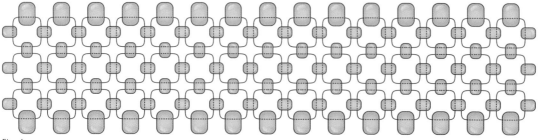

Fig. 6

2. Continue in right angle weave to close the flat beadwork into a loop by adding an 11°, a 15°, a 15°, and an 11°.

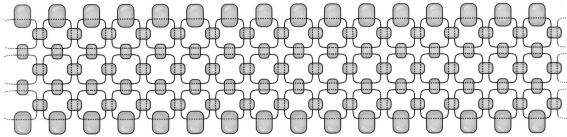

Fig. 7

3. Fold the 11°s of the opposing edges together and continue in right angle weave to add a row of 3mm crystals or 8° round seed beads—as the project specifies—and close the tube.

Fig. 8

BEZELED CRYSTAL ROUND STONES

Capture a crystal stone with the tight hug of a one-drop right angle weave bezel. Projects incorporate components in a variety of ways. The number of rows wide and units long will vary with the stone size.

27mm round stone

1. Work a strip of flat one-drop right angle weave three rows wide and 29 units long with 15° and 11° round seed beads. Row 1 is 15°s and 11°s, row 2 is 11°s, and row 3 is 11°s and 15°s.

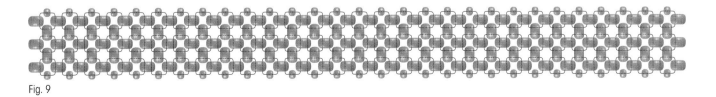

Fig. 9

2. Close the strip into a loop with two 15°s and two 11°s.

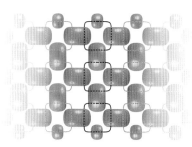

Fig. 10

3. Add 30 15°s between the 15°s in row 1, making a complete circle with the stitch path. This is the back of the bezel. Place the crystal into the bezel. Add 30 15°s between the 15°s in row 3, cinching up the row as you make a complete circle with the stitch path. Reinforce the 15° rounds in row 1 and row 3 as needed.

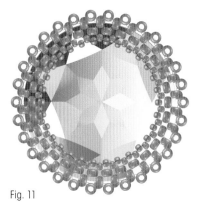

Fig. 11

12MM RIVOLI CHATON

1. Work a strip of flat one-drop right angle two rows wide and 13 units long with 15° and 11° round seed beads (see figure 12).Close the strip into a loop with two 15°s and one 11° (see figure 13).

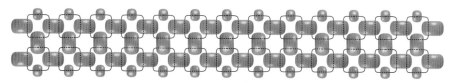

Fig. 12

12mm round stone

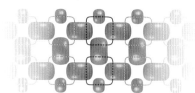

Fig. 13

2. Repeat the last step as for a 27mm stone, save for adding only 14 15°s to the front and 14 15°s to the back for the final cinch.

3. Use the same method to bezel a 12mm rivoli chaton except that the initial strip is 19 units long and closed with the 20th unit. Add 20 15°s to the front and 20 to the back.

CUBOIDS

In geometry speak, a cuboid is a solid that has six rectangular faces at right angles to each other. For our purposes, cuboids are cool components to use in our projects, resembling an ice cream sandwich made of beads. Yum! Use this technique to complete the Voldekol Necklace, Seussical Earrings, Karin Cuff, and Chiclets Bracelet. Cuboids made using traditional cubic right angle weave require more beads, thread, and time. Bind the inner beads or outer beads first, as you prefer or as the project necessitates.

RULE 1
Cuboids are made of two faces—two pieces of one-drop right angle weave exactly the same number of units wide and long.

RULE 2
Cuboids are three units wide.

RULE 3
Cuboids are an odd number of units long.

RULE 4
Bind cuboid edges by stitching in right angle weave around the four edges and borrowing one bead from each face.

RULE 5
Bind the cuboid by stitching together the corresponding front and back beads of the even units in the middle rows of both faces—i.e., units 2, 4, 6, etc.

RULE 6
Attach one-drop tubular peyote by stitching through the left and right beads of the even units in the middle row of either face—i.e., units 2, 4, 6, etc.

RULE 7
Cuboids can be executed in traditional cubic right angle weave, if desired.

INNER BINDING

Hold together two faces of right angle weave that are an odd number of units long and three units wide. The example is seven units long. Bind the top face to the bottom face at six points identified by the blue, green, and purple beads. In a circular motion, stitch through the first set of single blue beads from each face, then the second set of single blue beads (blue lines). Repeat to bind the green (green lines) and purple beads (purple lines).

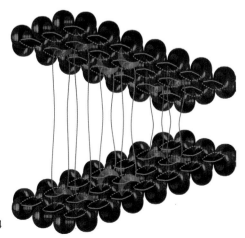

Fig. 14

Simply continue in right angle weave to bind all four corresponding edges of the two faces. Begin at any point and, continuing in right angle weave, incorporate beads from the top face edge (red beads) and the bottom face edge (blue beads) while adding one new bead at a time (green beads).

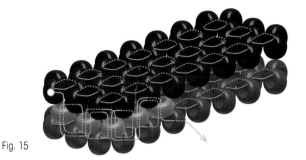

Fig. 15

BIND TWO FACES

In many projects you have the option of binding two faces of flat right angle weave together. Of course, you can often replace the binding with traditional cubic right angle weave, which will require additional time, beads, and stitching.

Align two right angle weave faces. Continuing in right angle weave, bind the faces together by adding one additional bead at a time to all of the units, except for the first unit, which uses two beads.

Tubular One-Drop Even-Count Peyote Stitch

Tubular peyote is at the heart of this book's projects, and reinforcing each row gives it body. If each row is not reinforced, a mushy and weak piece of beadwork will result. These projects use a simple version of tubular peyote stitch with two beads in each row. Each row is finite, meaning that there is a step up at the end of each row that becomes the start of the next row. Like any other form of peyote, the first run of beads becomes rows 1 and 2. There are many forms of peyote—the most basic being the flat, even-count form that is not used in any of these projects.

Note: Though the word *string* is used, each bead is counted as being added with a single stitch, and stitch counts include every pass made through each individual bead.

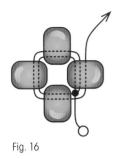

Fig. 16

ROWS 1 AND 2

String four beads and, leaving a 6-inch (15 cm) tail, tie a double overhand knot, then stitch through the first bead added, the second bead added, the third bead added, the fourth bead added, and the first bead added. Nine stitches complete the row. See figure 16.

ROW 3

String one bead and stitch through the third bead added previously, string one bead and stitch through the first bead added previously, the first bead just added, the third bead added previously, the second bead just added, the first bead added previously, and the first bead just added. Nine stitches complete the row. See figure 17.

ROW 4, EVEN ROW

String one bead and stitch through the second bead previously added, string one bead and stitch through the first bead previously added, the first bead just added, the second bead previously added, the second bead just added, the first bead previously added, and the first bead just added. Nine stitches complete the row. See figure 18.

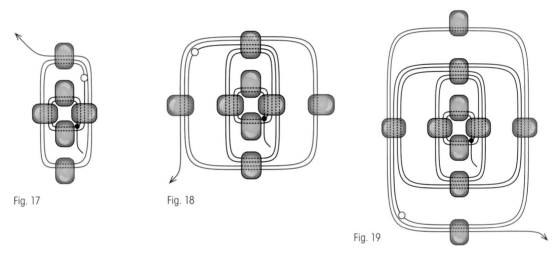

Fig. 17   Fig. 18

Fig. 19

ROW 5, ODD ROW

String one bead and stitch through the second bead previously added, string one bead and stitch through the first bead previously added, the first bead just added, the second bead previously added, the second bead just added, the first bead previously added, and the first bead just added. Nine stitches complete the row.

Repeat even and odd rows to the desired length. See figure 19.

COUNTERCLOCKWISE VERSUS CLOCKWISE STITCHING

There are two principles to remember when working with tubular even-count peyote stitch with only two beads in each row.

PRINCIPLE 1

Your dominant hand determines the direction.

When working lengths of tubular peyote stitch, it is significant which direction the needle and thread travel as beads are added to the tube end. Typically, it is the ergonomic choice of a right-handed individual to travel counterclockwise and of a left-handed individual to travel clockwise.

PRINCIPLE 2

Always stitch in the same direction.

From the beginning of a project to completion, no matter which end of a tube it is, always stitch in the same direction. If there are several lengths of tubular peyote, maintain uniformity between them by completing them all with stitches going in the same direction. Take up a peyote tube, and you'll see two ends from which to continue working. Beadwork may resume from either end, but remember to continue stitching in the same direction as previously.

PRINCIPLE 3

Peyote stitched consistently in one direction will appear to twist slightly in the opposite direction.

Reward follows your hard work and attention when you follow the first two principles: Your beadwork exhibits the opposite twist. For example, if you execute beadwork in a counterclockwise manner, it exhibits a clockwise twist.

FINISHING AND ADDING THREAD

This method is similar to working with right angle weave as described above in that half-hitch knots are used in a way to keep them hidden and applied in a quantity to ensure that threads will not come undone. A thread needs to be finished off when it is approximately 6 inches (15 cm) long and a new working thread should be approximately fingertip to fingertip with your arms outstretched in length. Stitch through an adjacent bead, pull the thread completely through, stitch under adjacent threads, and very neatly pull up the loop. Before the loop closes from tension, stitch through it and the next adjacent bead—effectively pulling the half-hitch knot into the bead. Repeat to create a total of three knots—two are shown. If finishing a thread, cut it. If adding a thread, continue to stitch until reaching the point where beadwork continues. See figure 20.

PEYOTE BEAD

A peyote bead can originate from a four-bead ring or from the end of a one-drop peyote tube. In both cases, always work with a single thread, and reinforce every row. Peyote beads are typically made with 11° round seed beads, but can be made with other sizes of round seed beads. Rounds 1 (green beads) and 2 (blue beads) are the last two rows of a peyote tube or the four-bead ring. See figure 21.

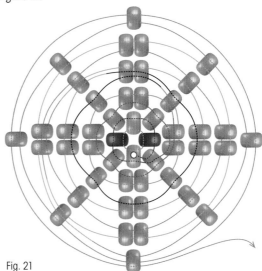

Fig. 20

Fig. 21

ROUND 3, INCREASE, RED LINE

Exit the needle and thread from the first bead in, one round back. String a bead and stitch through the first bead in the last round—the next bead sticking up. String a bead and stitch through the second bead in the second round back. String a bead and stitch through the third bead in the last round—the next bead sticking up. String a bead and stitch again through the first bead in, one round back. Reinforce the row by repeating the thread path again. Step up by stitching through the first bead added in the current round (red line).

ROUND 4, INCREASE, BLUE LINE

String two beads and stitch through the next bead sticking out from round 3. Repeat three more times. Reinforce the round. Step up through the first two beads added in the round.

ROUND 5, GREEN LINE

String one bead and stitch through the next two beads sticking out from the previous round. Repeat three more times. Reinforce the round. Step up through the first bead added in the round.

ROUND 6, BLACK LINE

String two beads and stitch through the next bead sticking out from the previous round. Repeat three more times. Reinforce the round. Step up through the first two beads added in the round.

ROUND 7, GOLD LINE

Repeat round 5.

ROUND 8, PURPLE LINE

Repeat round 6.

ROUND 9, PINK LINE

Repeat round 5.

ROUNDS 10 AND 11, DECREASE

String one bead and stitch through the next bead sticking out from round 9. Repeat three more times. Reinforce the row. Step up through the first bead added in the round.

CINCH

Stitch through the four beads added in rounds 10 and 11. Reinforce the row.

TWINKLE DROP

This is a versatile and beautiful drop that incorporates a bezeled rivoli chaton and a crystal drop with 11's and 3.4mm drop seed beads. Use it as an earring or a lush weight at the end of tubular peyote fringe. See Bezeled Crystal Round Stones for directions (page 13).

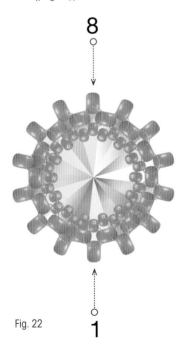

Fig. 22

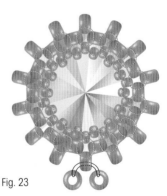

Fig. 23

Bezel a 12mm rivoli chaton crystal. Identify positions 1 and 8. See figure 22.

Exit the thread from position 1 at the widest edge of the bezel circumference. String one bead and stitch back through bead 1. String one bead and stitch back through position 1. Stitch back through the first bead just added, position 1, the second bead just added, position 1, and the first bead just added. See figure 23.

Use the beads added in the previous step to make a partial peyote bead. Red line: Continuing counterclockwise, string one bead, pass through the second bead just added, string one bead, and pass through the first bead just added. Reinforce the row and step up. Blue line: String one bead, pass through the second bead added at position 1, string one bead, pass through the second bead just added, string one bead, pass through the first bead added at position 1, string one bead, and pass through the first beaded just added. Reinforce the row and step up. Green line: String two beads, stitch through the first bead added with the blue line, string two beads, stitch through the second bead added with the blue line, string two beads, stitch through the third bead added with the blue line, string two beads, and stitch through the fourth bead added with the blue line. Reinforce the row and step up. See figure 24.

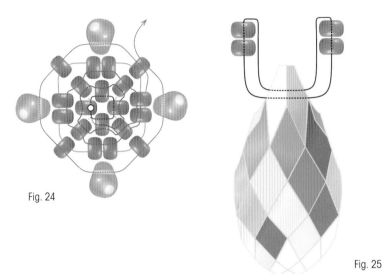

Fig. 24

Fig. 25

Black line (figure 25): Stitch in the crystal drop between sets of two beads added with the green line. Gold line: String one bead and stitch through the first set of two beads just added and repeat three more times. Rein-force the row and step up. Lavender line: String one drop, stitch through the first bead just added, string one drop, stitch through the second bead just added, string one drop, stitch through the third bead just added, string one drop, and stitch through the fourth bead just added. Reinforce the row.

Stitch Interplay

The most creative moments in beadwork occur when you either have knowledge and willingness to experiment or are simply unafraid of failure. Try these varying combinations of right angle weave and peyote stitch for an unlimited supply of possibilities.

BUILD TUBULAR PEYOTE FROM RIGHT ANGLE WEAVE

Use this method to build a section of tubular peyote up from an existing piece of one-drop right angle weave. I'm going to describe a counterclockwise thread path, though it may also be performed clockwise. The blue and green beads are simply representative; of course, you should be using the colors chosen for the project! Employ this technique to build the Karin Cuff or any other time tubular peyote is joined to right angle weave.

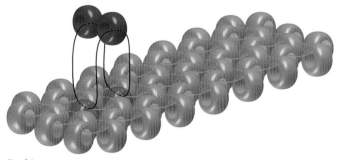

Fig. 26

Exit the left green bead of the right angle weave face, string a blue bead, pass through the right green bead of the face, string the second blue bead, pass through the first green bead again, repeat the stitches to secure, and step up through the first blue bead added. See figure 26.

Continue in tubular peyote, counting the blue beads just added as round 1.

ATTACH EXISTING TUBULAR PEYOTE TO RIGHT ANGLE WEAVE

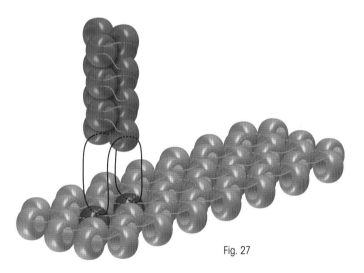

Fig. 27

Use this method to attach a section of existing tubular peyote to an existing piece of one-drop right angle weave. I'm going to describe a counterclockwise thread path as you work from the tube toward the face, though it may be performed in a clockwise direction. The blue and green beads are simply representative; of course, you should be using the colors chosen for the project! Use this technique to complete the Trispire Necklace, Voldekol Necklace, Karin Cuff, and others.

Exit the needle and thread left from the front green bead at the peyote tube end. Stitch toward the back through the left blue bead, stitch through the back green bead at the peyote tube end going toward the right, stitch forward through the right blue bead, repeat the thread path, and weave in the thread or go on to the next operation as needed. See figure 27.

BUILD RIGHT ANGLE WEAVE FROM TUBULAR PEYOTE

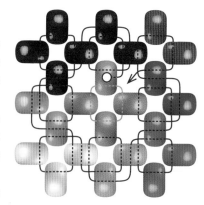

We do a substantial amount of attaching tubular peyote to right angle weave or beginning a tube of peyote up from a face of right angle weave, but sometimes it makes sense to add right angle weave off the end of a peyote tube. This method can be used to add a face of right angle weave from any two sequential rows of tubular peyote.

Identify the last row and second-to-last row of tubular peyote. This is significant because these two rows are referred to a number of times. In figure 28, the gray beads represent the last two rows of tubular peyote—the top and bottom beads are the last row and the left and right beads are the second-to-last row. Please note that this method of adding right angle weave can begin by stitching through any of the beads in the last two rows and going in either direction. The steps that follow are only one of a number of ways this technique can be executed. The reinforcing of each bead unit is included in the text.

Fig. 28

UNIT 1
Exit the needle and thread out the right side of the top bead (gray) in the last peyote row. String three beads (fuchsia). Working counterclockwise, pass through the gray bead last exited, the three beads just added, the gray bead, and the three beads just added again. The thread will exit the third bead just added.

UNIT 2
String three beads (red). Continuing clockwise in right angle weave, pass through the third bead added in unit 1, the three beads just added, the unit 1 bead, and the first bead just added.

UNIT 3
String two beads (orange). Working counterclockwise, pass up through the left bead of the second-to-last peyote tube row (gray), the first bead added in unit 2, the two beads just added, the peyote tube bead, the unit 2 bead, and the two beads just added.

UNIT 4
String three beads (yellow). Working clockwise, pass through the second bead added in unit 3, the three beads just added, the second bead added in unit 3, and the first bead just added.

UNIT 5
String two beads (chartreuse). Working counterclockwise, pass left through the bottom bead of the last peyote row, the first bead added in unit 4, the two beads just added, the peyote bead, the unit 4 bead, and both beads just added.

UNIT 6
String three beads (green). Working clockwise, pass through the second bead added in unit 5, the three beads just added, the second bead added in unit 5, and the first bead just added.

UNIT 7
String two beads (blue). Working counterclockwise, pass down through the right bead of the second-to-last peyote tube row (gray), the first bead added in unit 6, the two beads just added, the peyote bead, the unit 6 bead, both beads just added, and then stitch up through the rightmost bead of unit 1.

UNIT 8
String two beads (purple). Working clockwise, pass through the second bead added in unit 7, the rightmost bead of unit 1 (fuchsia), the two beads just added, the unit 7 bead, and the unit 1 bead.

Weave the thread to begin the next operation or weave it in.

Finishing Touches

Here are a few shorter, simpler techniques to put the finishing touches on the projects you've worked so hard to produce. Take care to make strong connections for lasting results.

CLOSED JUMP RING

These ingenious little findings provide an immense amount of longevity to beadwoven jewelry. These wire rings are soldered closed. Closed rings are directly and securely attached to the beadwork, and can then be connected by open jump rings to attach to clasps and other components.

Attach a closed jump ring to the end of tubular peyote by stitching through the first end bead from right to left, the closed jump ring, the second end bead from right to left, and the closed jump ring, and repeat to the desired strength (figure 29).

Attach a closed jump ring to the surface of right angle weave by stitching down through the first red dot bead, through the soldered jump ring, through the second red dot bead, and down through the first red dot bead. Repeat to the desired strength (figure 30).

Fig. 29

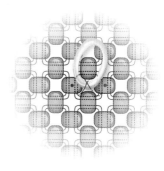

Fig. 30

OPEN JUMP RING AND EAR WIRES

To open a jump ring, hold a pair of chain-nose pliers in each hand. Grasp the jump ring close to the opening with the pliers in your nondominant hand. These pliers should simply hold the jump ring steady for the rest of the operation. Next, grasp the jump ring on the other side of the opening with the pliers in your dominant hand and twist the ring open. Slip the open jump ring through the loops you desire to connect and twist it closed with

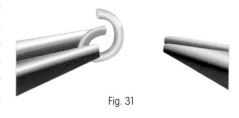

Fig. 31

the pliers in your dominant hand. Ear wires are opened and closed in the same manner. Grasp the ear wire in your nondominant hand and manipulate the ear wire ring with the pliers in your dominant hand.

Chapter 1

NECKLACES

CATKIN NECKLACE

Peyote beads bobble and spiral like catkins found on poplar and birch trees. Wrap the necklace around your wrist, too.

OVERVIEW

Make a profusion of components in three colors, then connect them with tubular peyote in the fourth color bead. Reinforce every round.

COMPONENTS

Each component is worked in a main color—A, B, or C—with three rows of D in the middle. Make 24 components in each color.

Fig. 1

Cut a 4-foot (1.2 m) length of thread. String four beads, tie a double overhand knot, and reinforce—these are rounds 1 and 2. Continue from round 3 through the cinch to make a peyote bead. Build three rounds of tubular peyote from two opposing beads in the cinch in the main color, three rounds of D, and five rounds of the main color. Build a peyote bead in the main color beginning at round 3 and finishing at the cinch. Set aside.

FINISHING

All components are connected in a continuous necklace with four-round lengths of tubular peyote. Each component will be rotated approximately 90° from the previous component.

Red line: Build four tubular peyote rounds up from two Ds at the middle of a component.

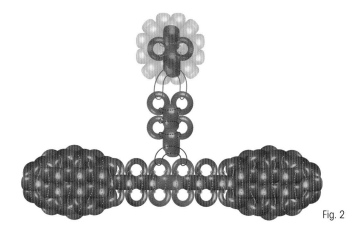

Fig. 2

Blue line: Continuing in tubular peyote, stitch the last two Ds added to the middle Ds of a new component. Repeat the red and blue lines until all components are joined in this order:

*Six A components, one B, one A, one B, one A, one B, one A, six Bs, one C, one B, one C, one B, one C, one B, six Cs, one A, one C, one A, one C, one A, and one C. Repeat from * one more time.

Hold the necklace from one end and allow it to hang naturally—remembering principle 3 of tubular peyote stitch. This long length of tubular peyote will rotate around a number of times.

Add four rounds of tubular peyote in D. Connect the last round of D to the first A and reinforce.

SUPPLIES

Beadweaving kit

Size 11° round seed beads:

A, matte fuchsia, 21 grams

B, matte olive, 21 grams

C, matte aqua, 21 grams

D, bronze metallic, 9 grams

Gold thread

TECHNIQUES

Peyote bead

Tubular peyote

FINISHED LENGTH

25 inches (63.5 cm)

LUBLINEA NECKLACE

SUPPLIES

Beadweaving kit

Size 11° round seed beads:

A, opaque black, 10 grams

B, opaque olive matte, 2 grams

C, fuchsia matte, 2 grams

D, aqua matte, 2 grams

Size 15° round black opaque seed beads, 4 grams

4mm jet AB2X bicone crystals, 252

Black thread

TECHNIQUES

Tubular peyote

Right angle weave ring

FINISHED LENGTH

40 inches (101.6 cm)

This necklace, made up of a line of loops, sparkles in all the right places.

OVERVIEW

Six three-ring sets made of right angle weave and tubular peyote are connected with lengths of tubular peyote.

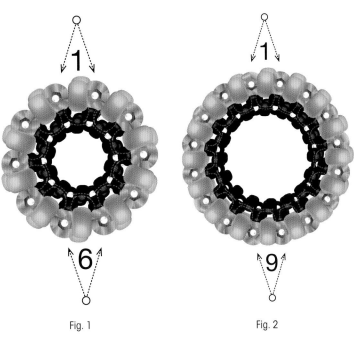

Fig. 1   Fig. 2

Fig. 3

RINGS

Make six sets of rings. Each set of rings consists of one large ring flanked by two small ones. Weave in extra threads or reserve them for the short peyote tube attachments between rings.

Small

Make a right angle weave ring that begins with 9×3 units of 11°s and 15°s in the first step and follows exactly the second and third steps. Make four rings each using B, C, and D for the 11°s. See figure 1.

Large

Make a right angle weave ring as specified in "Fundamentals" that begins with 16×3 units of 11°s and 15°s in the first step and follows exactly the second and third steps. Make four rings each using B, C, and D for the 11°s. See figure 2.

COMPONENT

Stitch three rows of A in tubular peyote starting from the unit 6 crystals of a small ring. Stitch the third row of the tubular peyote to the unit 1 crystals of a large ring. Weave the thread through the large ring beadwork. Stitch three rows of A in tubular peyote starting from the unit 9 crystals of the large ring. Stitch the third row of the tubular peyote to the unit 1 crystals of a small ring. See figure 3.

FINAL LINKING

Take up a three-ring set and stitch 100 rows of A in tubular peyote to the unit 6 crystals of the bottom small ring. Stitch the 100th row to the unit 1 crystals of the top small ring of the second three-ring set. Repeat to incorporate all six sets. Stitch the last peyote row of the sixth three-ring set to the unit 1 crystals of the top small ring of the first three-ring set.

Remember principle 3 of this type of tubular peyote: Allow the length to twist, and only then secure the length to the cuboid—each length will twist around approximately two times.

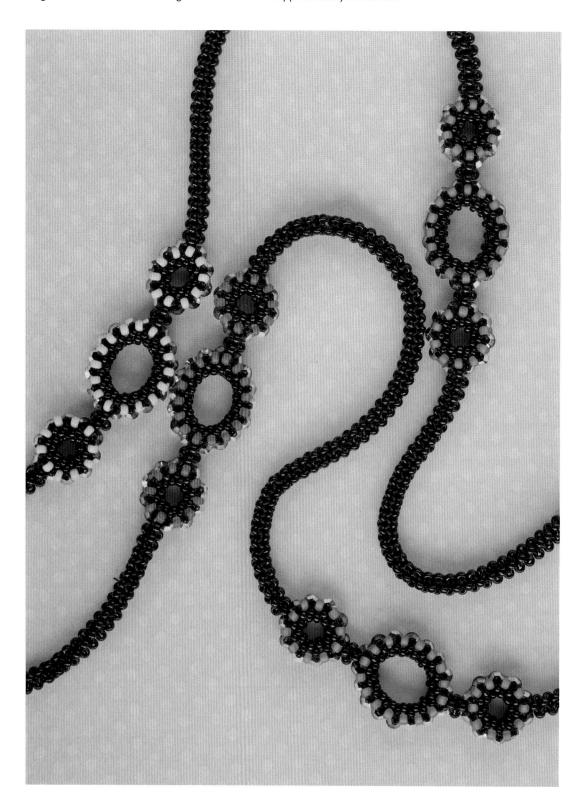

MARSEEAH NECKLACE

SUPPLIES

Beadweaving kit

Size 11° bright orange opaque round seed beads, 29 grams

Size 15° bright orange opaque round seed beads, 2 grams

3.4mm silver-lined chartreuse drop beads, 114

27mm crystal AB article #1201 crystal round stone, 1

18mm crystal AB article #1122 crystal round stone rivoli chaton, 1

12mm crystal AB article #1122 crystal round stone rivoli chaton, 3

8.5×17mm #6010 crystal AB pendant, 3

TECHNIQUES

Bezeled crystal round stones

Tubular peyote

Wavy chain

Fancy drops

Add two to one

FINISHED LENGTH

32 inches (81 cm)

This crazy necklace makes my friend laugh because it is bright orange, so it is named after her—the phonetic pronunciation of her real name, Marcia, that is.

OVERVIEW

A continuous length of wavy chain with a simple drop bead embellishment captures the large and medium bezeled crystal stones to create a centerpiece. Three drops are added to the pendant.

WAVY CHAIN

Stitch two continuous lengths of 11°s in modified right angle weave. Bind them together in right angle weave to form a substantial chain and embellish.

Base

Follow the alternating clockwise and counterclockwise thread path of right angle weave with only three sides of beads, rather than the usual four. Reinforce each unit with a second pass. Units 1–6 are a set.

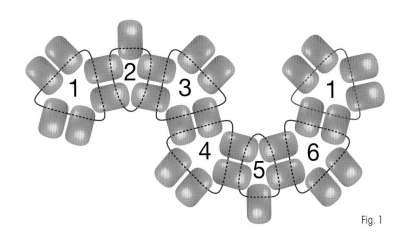

Fig. 1

UNIT 1
String six beads, tie a knot to weave in later, and pass through all beads again.

UNIT 2
Add three beads to two beads from the first unit.

UNIT 3
Add four beads to two beads from the second unit.

UNIT 4
Add four beads to two beads from the third unit.

UNIT 5
Add three beads to two beads from the fourth unit.

UNIT 6
Add four beads to two beads from the fifth unit.

Add a modified unit 1 to unit 6 adding only four beads (blue line)*.

Repeat from unit 2 to the asterisk and make the base 66 sets long. Attach the 66th set (blue dots) to the first set (red dots) with a 67th set (green line). See figure 2.

Repeat to make a second base.

Fig. 2

Bind and Embellish

Line up the two bases and bind all edge units with 11°s (red lines). Secure a 3.4mm drop to the edge of unit 2 in each division—except for three consecutive sets. Leave these units open to add fringe and curve against the bottom of the 27mm bezeled stone.

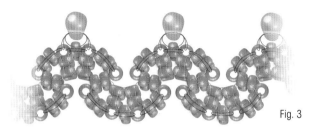

Fig. 3

CENTERPIECE

Bezel and embellish two stones. Then, strategically attach them to the wavy chain, which will flow around them.

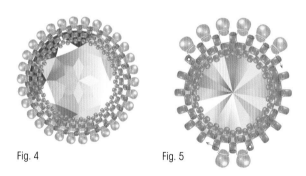

Fig. 4   Fig. 5

27mm Stone

Bezel the stone and, with a doubled thread, embellish with 30 drops. See figure 4.

18mm Stone

Bezel the stone and, with a doubled thread, embellish in the middle ditch with six drops on top and two drops on the bottom. See figure 5.

CONNECT THE BEZELS TO THE WAVY CHAIN

Align the three unembellished sets of the Wavy Chain against the bezeled 27mm stone. Select a right angle weave unit of the bezel, and exit the thread from the leftmost 11° (red dot). As in tubular peyote, bind two bezel beads to the front and back of unit 2 of the wavy chain 11°s (red line). Repeat until the connection is secure. Repeat to connect at the blue lines. Attach the 18mm stone by passing through the green dot bead, the leftmost unit 2 bead, the green dot bead, the rightmost unit 2 bead, and repeating until secure. Attach at three additional points indicated with green thread.

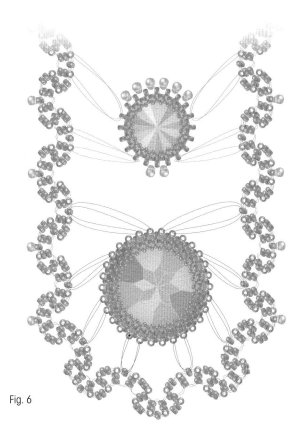

Fig. 6

FRINGE

This necklace just wouldn't be the same without the bauble and bling fancy drops added. Make three fancy drops. Set two aside.

Use the add two to one technique to attach two 11°s to position 8 (see figure 22 on page 19). Add 13 more rows of tubular peyote to the two beads just added. Connect the 13th row to two 11°s of the first unembellished unit of wavy chain as if they were the 14th row. Repeat to add fringe to the wavy chain at the second and third unembellished units.

MOTHER'S MEDITATION NECKLACE

SUPPLIES

Beadweaving kit

Size 11° round seed
  beads:
  A, opaque olive
    matte, 4 grams
  B, orange-lined
    topaz, 4 grams
  C, matte dark
    aqua, 4 grams
  D, opaque red AB,
    4 grams
  E, bronze metallic,
    17 grams
Red thread

TECHNIQUES

Tubular one-drop
  even-count peyote
Peyote bead

FINISHED
LENGTH

60 inches (1.5 m)

Made entirely of tubular peyote lengths and beads, this necklace features 40 beaded beads that represent the 40 weeks of gestation. This piece was designed for expectant mothers and other family members to enjoy while anticipating the birth of a child—but, of course, everyone can enjoy this project.

OVERVIEW

Remember principle 3 of this type of tubular peyote: Allow the length to twist, and only then secure the length to the first peyote bead.

LENGTH WITH PEYOTE BEADS

1

Make a peyote bead in A. Stitch 25 rounds of E in tubular peyote from the cinch row.

2

Stitch two more rounds of tubular peyote with Bs. Continue to build a peyote bead with Bs at round 3, as the last two rounds of tubular peyote are rounds 1 and 2 of the peyote bead. Stitch 25 rounds of E in tubular peyote up from the cinch row.

3

Stitch two more rounds of tubular peyote with Cs. Continue to build a peyote bead with Cs at round 3, as the last two rounds of tubular peyote are rounds 1 and 2 of the peyote bead. Stitch 25 rounds of E in tubular peyote up from the cinch row.

4

Stitch two more rounds of tubular peyote with Ds. Continue to build a peyote bead with Ds at round 3, as the last two rounds of tubular peyote are rounds 1 and 2 of the peyote bead. Stitch 25 rounds of E in tubular peyote up from the cinch row.

5

Stitch two more rounds of tubular peyote with As. Continue to build a peyote bead with As at round 3, as the last two rounds of tubular peyote are rounds 1 and 2 of the peyote bead. Stitch 25 rounds of Es in tubular peyote up from the cinch row.

Repeat steps 2–5 two more times, then steps 2–4 one more time. There will be ten peyote beads of each color with each separated by 25 rounds of tubular peyote, ending with 25 rounds of tubular peyote.

Stitch the 25th row of tubular peyote to the first round of As in the first peyote bead, taking care to allow the overall length to spiral naturally.

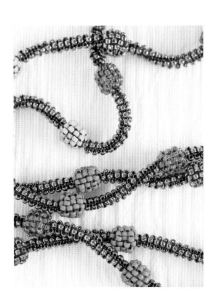

OBSESSION NECKLACE

A woman's ring set off an obsession with gold and turquoise, resulting in this necklace and a gorgeous gold and turquoise ring from my wonderful, observant husband for my 40th birthday.

OVERVIEW

Make fancy right angle weave faces. Bind the faces together, embellish with bezeled rivoli chatons, and finish with a chain made of tubular peyote rings. The big bonus of the stretchy nature of the chain is that there is no clasp!

CENTERPIECE

There are three phases of making the centerpiece: make the base, bezel the stones, and add them all together.

Centerpiece Base

Stitch a face with six arches and six partial arches using 11° and 15° beads and plain old one-drop right angle weave. Repeat to stitch a second face. See figure 1.

Sandwich the two faces together and bind all inner and outer edges. Bind all units with 11°s unless binding a 15°, then use a 15° to bind the two faces. See figure 2.

Fig. 1

Fig. 2

Bezeled Stones

Encase the six stones with right angle weave bezels made with size 11° and 15° seed beads.

Attach the Stones to the Base

Work a set of red, black, and blue dots, then attach the following set. See figure 3.

Stitch the red dot beads on the back of a bezel to the corresponding red dot beads on the top face of the centerpiece. Stitch the black dot beads on the back of a

Fig. 3

Beadweaving kit

Size 8° gold metallic AB round seed beads, 16 grams

Size 11° opaque turquoise round seed beads, 21 grams

Size 15° gold metallic round seed beads, 4 grams

12mm crystal AB article #1122 crystal round stone rivoli chaton, 6

Gold thread

TECHNIQUES

Right angle weave

Bind two faces

Bezeled round crystal stones

Tubular peyote

FINISHED LENGTH

20 inches (50.8 cm)

bezel to the corresponding black dot beads on the centerpiece. Stitch the blue dot beads on the back of a bezel to the corresponding blue dot beads on the centerpiece.

CHAIN

Make a chain of links 40 rows of tubular peyote long—odd rows are made of two 11°s and even rows of one 8° and one 15°. All links are 40 rows long. Remember to make the chain long enough to stretch over your head, as there is no clasp.

INITIAL LOOP, ROWS 1 AND 2, RED LINE

String one of each to begin a peyote tube: 8°, 11°, 15°, and 11°. Tie a knot, reinforce, and stitch through the 8° again to step up and begin the next row.

ROW 3, BLUE LINE

String an 11° and pass through the 15° in the initial ring. String an 11° and pass through the 8° in the initial ring. Reinforce and step up through the first 11° added in the row.

ROW 4, GREEN LINE

String a 15° and pass through the second 11° added in the previous row. String an 8° and pass through the first 11° added in the previous row. Reinforce and step up through the 15°.

ROW 5, BLACK LINE

String an 11° and pass through the 8° added in the previous row. String an 11° and pass through the 15° added in the previous row. Reinforce and step up through the first 11° added in the row.

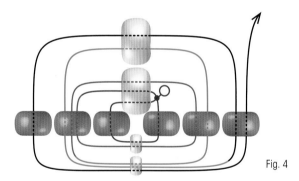

Fig. 4

ROWS 6–40

Continue in tubular peyote stitch to complete 40 rows.

Continue in tubular peyote to join the 40th row to the first row. See figure 5.

Make the next link. Before securing it closed, fish one end through the previous link and stitch the 40th row to the first row. See figure 6.

Fig. 5

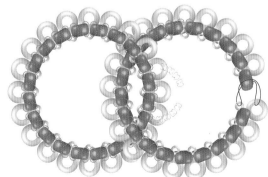

Fig. 6

Continue in this manner to make 29 connected chain links. Before closing the 30th link, connect it through a small opening in the pendant, then secure it closed. Make a 31st link and, before closing, connect it through an adjacent small opening in the pendant, then secure it closed as in figure 6.

TRISPIRE NECKLACE

SUPPLIES

Beadweaving kit

8° matte teal round
   seed beads,
   25 grams

11° matte chartreuse
   round seed beads,
   20 grams

15° transparent
   fuchsia round
   seed beads,
   5 grams

3mm jet AB2X
   bicone crystals, 74

Gold thread

TECHNIQUES

Flat right angle
   weave

Right angle weave
   edge join

Tubular one-drop
   even-count peyote

Building tubular
   peyote from right
   angle weave

Embellishing right
   angle weave

FINISHED
LENGTH

19 inches (48 cm)

Spiraling lengths of peyote are finished with a unique right angle weave and peyote closure. Inspired by my brother, Dr. Joel Nelson.

OVERVIEW

Force tubular peyote to spiral by using three different seed bead sizes. Each spiral is a different length for a graduated effect. The necklace is finished with a multistrand clasp.

Note: The steps of creating this project are broken down into finite sections for the purpose of presentation; however, the method of organization may not represent how you prefer to work. I recommend beginning with the separate steps as they are written and assembling them in your own fashion.

STRANDS

The body of the necklace is made up of three separate strands of beadwork. Work each strand in tubular even-count peyote stitch with two beads added in each row. In one row, two 11°s are added, and in the other row one 8° and one 15° are added. Use a single thread, weave it in, and add a new thread as needed. Begin with the inside (shortest) strand. Make the second strand 1 inch (2.5 cm) longer than the first strand. Make the third strand 1 inch (2.5 cm) longer than the second strand.

FIGURE 1, ROWS 1 AND 2

String one 11°, one 15°, one 11°, and one 8°. Tie a double overhand knot, leaving a 6-inch (15 cm) tail to weave in later; stitch through all beads again and the first 11° strung.

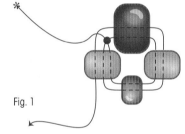

Fig. 1

FIGURE 2, ROW 3

String one 15° and stitch through the next 11° from the previous row. String one 8° and stitch through the next 11° from the previous row. Stitch through the 15° just added, the 11° from the previous row, the 8° just added, and the 11° from the previous row. Step up through the 15° to begin the next row.

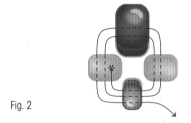

Fig. 2

FIGURE 3, ROW 4

String one 11° and stitch through the 8° in the previous row. String one 11° and stitch through the 15° in the previous row. Stitch through the first 11° just added, the 8° from the previous row, the second 11° just added, and the 15° from the previous row. Step up through the first 11° in this row to begin the next row.

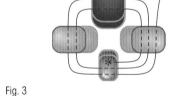
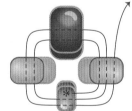

Fig. 3

FIGURE 4, ROW 5

String one 8° and stitch through the next 11° from the previous row. String one 15° and stitch through the next 11° from the previous row. Stitch through the 8° just added, the 11° from the previous row, the 15° just added, and the 11° from the previous row. Step up through the 8° just added to begin the next row.

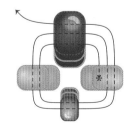

Fig. 4

FIGURE 5, ROW 6

String one 11° and stitch through the 15° in the previous row. String one 11° and stitch through the 8° in the previous row. Stitch through the first 11° just added, the 15° from the previous row, the second 11° just added, and the 8° from the previous row. Step up through the first 11° in this row to begin the next row.

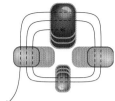

Fig. 5

Repeat rows 3–6 until the desired length is reached. Make sure each strand begins and ends with the two 11°s sticking up.

CLASP

The main structure of both clasp halves—eye and hook—are constructed with right angle weave. The three hooks are constructed with tubular even-count peyote stitch. The front faces of both halves are embellished with 15°s. Work with a single thread, finishing and adding thread as needed.

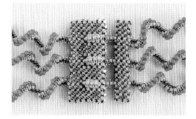

Eye Half

FIGURE 6

Work a base of one-drop right angle weave 14 units wide and six units tall, leaving three openings. Repeat to create a second, identical base for the eye half.

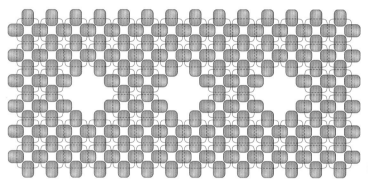

Fig. 6

For the hook half of the clasp, work two bases of one-drop right angle weave 14 units wide and two units tall.

FIGURE 7, EMBELLISHMENT

Embellish 60 units of right angle weave on the front of the eye half, each with a single 15°. Do not embellish the 12 units where the hooks will eventually make contact. Embellish all units of one hook base in the same manner.

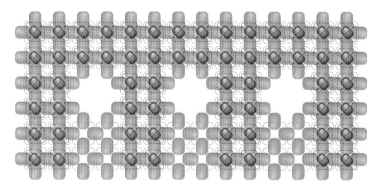

Fig. 7

FIGURE 8, BINDING

Use right angle weave and 3mm bicones to bind the embellished bases to the unembellished bases on both clasp halves. To complete the eye half, bind the three openings using 11°s.

Contacts

To create a landing area for the strand ends, add two 11°s at each anchor point.

FIGURE 9, EYE STRANDS

Identify the three areas where the contacts will be added.

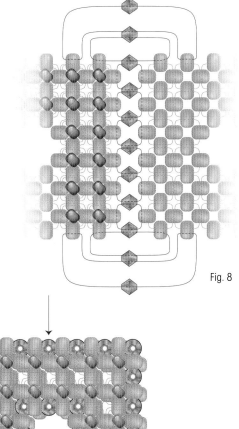

Fig. 8

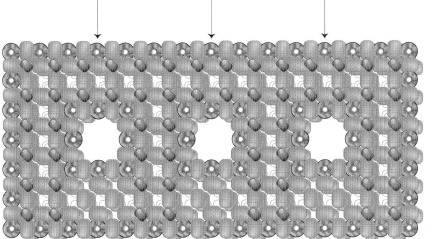

Fig. 9

FIGURE 10, CONTACTS

Add two 11°s (red line) between the third and fourth units on the edge, the seventh and eighth units on the edge, and the 11th and 12th units on the edge. Secure with at least two more passes.

Continuing in tubular even-count peyote stitch, bind the strand ends to the contacts with two or more passes (red arrows in figures 9 and 11).

Fig. 10

Hook Half

Add the contacts as in figure 10 to the units indicated by the red and blue arrows (figure 11). Add three even-count tubular peyote hooks to the contacts at the blue arrows.

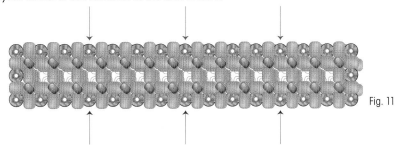

Fig. 11

FIGURE 12, ROW 1

Weave the thread to exit the top contact. String one 11°, then stitch through the bottom contact, string one 11°, then stitch through the top contact, the first 11° just added, the bottom contact, the second 11° just added, the top contact, and the first 11° just added.

Fig. 12

FIGURE 13, ROW 2

String one 11° and stitch through the 11° in the previous row. String one 11°, and stitch through the 11° in the previous row, the first 11° just added, the 11° in the previous row, the second 11° just added, the 11° in the previous row, and the first 11° just added.

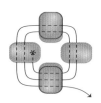

Fig. 13

FIGURE 14, ROW 3

String one 11° and stitch through the 11° in the previous row. String one 11° and stitch through the 11° in the previous row, the first 11° just added, the 11° in the previous row, the second 11° just added, the 11° in the previous row, and the first 11° just added.

Repeat rows 2 and 3 in series two more times.

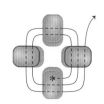

Fig. 14

FIGURE 15, ROW 8

Continuing in the same manner, add one 15° to the inside curve of the hook and one 11° to the outside curve of the hook.

Fig. 15

FIGURE 16, ROW 9

Add two 11°s.

Fig. 16

FIGURE 17, ROW 10

Add a 15° to the inside and an 11° to the outside.

Repeat the steps for rows 9 and 10 seven more times to complete 25 rows.

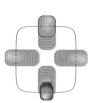

Fig. 17

FIGURE 18, HOOK FINISH

Beginning at the clasp base (red dots), double bind the beads inside the hook with a ladder stitch, and stitch toward the tip (blue dot). Add one 11° to the last two beads of the peyote tube to visually finish off the hook.

Repeat to add two more hooks to complete the clasp.

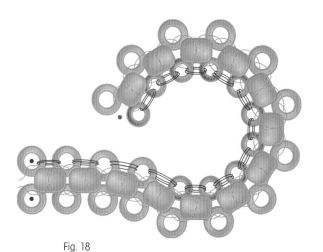

Fig. 18

VERTANN NECKLACE

The vibrant arts scene in Santa Cruz, California, is due in part to the efforts of one extraordinary person, who inspired this project. Ann Ostermann surrounds herself with vibrant shades of green and enthusiastically promotes creativity in my hometown.

OVERVIEW

Three ring and tubular peyote drop and bead components are linked into a centerpiece with tubular peyote and finished with peyote tube and bead lengths. Finish the project with a right angle weave ring and tubular peyote bead closure.

RIGHT ANGLE WEAVE RING

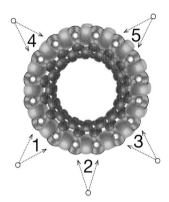

Fig. 1

Make three large rings. Stitch the first row with 11°s and 15°s, the second row with 15°s, and the third row with 15°s and 11°s. Close the tube with 16 crystal beads. Use these large rings for the front of the necklace. Set them aside. There are five positions for attaching. See figure 1.

Make one small ring. Stitch the first row with 11°s and 15°s, the second row with 15°s, and the third row with 15°s and 11°s. Close the tube with 13 crystal beads. Use the small ring for the clasp.

CENTERPIECE

Work three lengths of tubular peyote from the right angle weave ring edge, and weight the bottoms with peyote beads and a little embellishment. All peyote tubes will appear two rows shorter after adding a peyote bead.

Short Component

Make two of these components. Build a peyote bead with 11°s from the final two rows of all three tubular peyote lengths and embellish it with a crystal and a 15°. The peyote lengths are slightly shorter than those of the one large component. See figure 2.

SUPPLIES

Beadweaving kit

11° round opaque olive matte seed beads, 18 grams

15° round opaque green seed beads, <1 gram

3mm jet AB2X bicone crystal beads, 70

Gold thread

TECHNIQUES

Tubular one-drop even-count peyote

Peyote bead

Right angle weave ring

Peyote bead embellishment

Building tubular peyote from right angle weave

FINISHED LENGTH

17 inches (43 cm)

Fig. 2

POSITION 1

Stitch 24 rows of tubular peyote beginning from two crystals on the edge of the right angle weave ring (red line).

POSITION 2

Stitch 14 rows of tubular peyote beginning from two crystals on the edge of the right angle weave ring (blue line).

POSITION 3

This is a repeat of position 1.

Long Component

Make one of these components. Build a peyote bead with 11's from the final two rows of the tubular peyote lengths, and embellish them with a crystal and a 15°. The peyote lengths are slightly shorter than those of the two small components. See figure 3.

POSITION 1

Stitch 34 rows of tubular peyote to two crystals on the edge of the right angle weave ring (red line).

POSITION 2

Stitch 24 rows of tubular peyote to the next two crystals on the edge.

POSITION 3

This is a repeat of position 1.

Connecting

Create connections with tubular one-drop peyote stitch See figure 4.

Stitch seven rows of tubular peyote to the two crystals at position 4 on short component 1. Stitch the last two beads of the tube to two crystals at position 5 on the long component. Stitch seven rows of tubular peyote to the two crystals at position 4 on the long component, and stitch the last two beads of the tube to the two crystals at position 5 on short component 2.

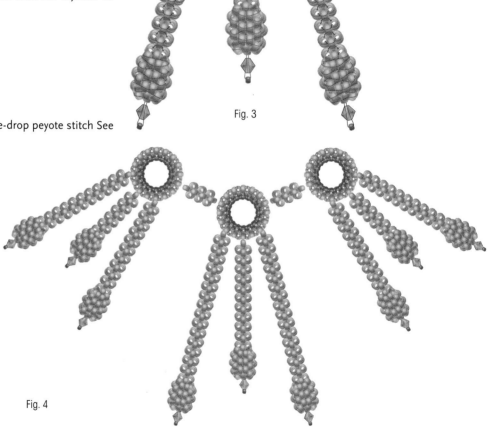

Fig. 3

Fig. 4

FINISHING

Make two lengths of tubular peyote with peyote beads with 11°s. Finish the first length with a final peyote bead and finish the second length by attaching the small right angle weave ring. Remember principle 3 of this type of tubular peyote and allow the length to twist.

Right Angle Weave Ring End

Stitch 14 rows of tubular peyote up from the two crystals at position 5 on short component 1. Build a peyote bead from the final two rows of tubular peyote. *Stitch 14 rows of tubular peyote to the peyote bead. Build a peyote bead from the final two rows of tubular peyote. Repeat from * five more times. Stitch six rows of tubular peyote. Stitch the last two rows of the tube to two crystals on the edge of the small right angle weave ring.

Peyote Bead End

Stitch 14 rows of tubular peyote up from the two crystals at position 4 on short component 2. Build a peyote bead from the final two rows of tubular peyote. *Stitch 14 rows of tubular peyote to two of the beads in the last row of the peyote bead. Build a peyote bead from the final two rows of tubular peyote. Repeat from * six more times.

VOLDEKOL NECKLACE

If rainbow were a color, it would be my favorite. Enjoy the free-form gradations from one vibrant color to the next. Second only to the fun colors is the seductive drape of the multiple strands.

OVERVIEW

Right angle weave cuboids give structure to nine strands of tubular peyote stitch gradated in two ways—changing bead colors and varied lengths. Finish the necklace with a customized toggle closure. Securely weave in the thread and trim it closely after attaching each component. Nubs of peyote give the impression of extending through the cuboids.

CUBOIDS

Make 20 cuboids, each in right angle weave with a single thread. Make two pieces of flat right angle weave with A and bind the edges with B. Bind the bead with a blue dot on the top right angle weave rectangle to the corresponding bead of the bottom right angle weave rectangle. Yellow numbers indicate positions. Weave in all threads and set aside.

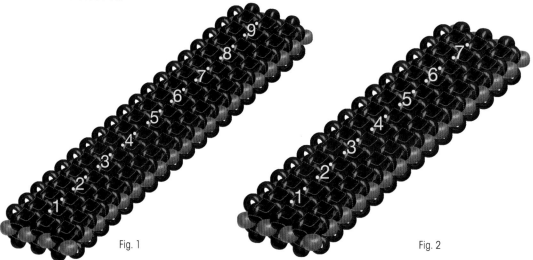

Fig. 1   Fig. 2

Cuboids 1 and 2, Figure 1

Make two pieces three units wide by 19 units long with A. Bind the middle row at positions 1–9 without adding beads. Continue in right angle weave to bind the edges with 44 Bs (blue lines).

Cuboids 3 and 4, Figure 2

Make two pieces three units wide by 15 units long with A. Bind the middle row at positions 1–7 without adding beads. Continue in right angle weave to bind the edges with 36 Bs (blue lines).

Cuboids 5 and 6, Figure 3

Make two pieces three units wide by 12 units long with A. Bind the middle row at positions 1–5 without adding beads. Continue in right angle weave to bind the edges with 28 Bs (blue lines).

Cuboids 7–20, Figure 4

Make two pieces three units wide by seven units long with A. Bind the middle row at positions 1–3 without adding beads. Continue in right angle weave to bind the edges with 20 Bs (blue lines).

Beadweaving kit

Size 11° round seed beads:
- A, opaque red rainbow, 43 grams
- B, opaque orange, 30 grams
- C, opaque yellow, 15 grams
- D, opaque chartreuse, 15 grams
- E, opaque green rainbow, 15 grams
- F, silver-lined blue zircon, 15 grams
- G, opaque royal blue, 15 grams
- H, transparent purple matte, 15 grams
- I, transparent fuchsia matte, 15 grams

Size 15° opaque orange round seed beads, 8 grams

Red thread

1-inch (2.5 cm) plastic ring

14-gauge copper wire, 1¼ inches (3.2 cm)

4mm round soldered 22-gauge jump rings, 12

4mm round open 22-gauge jump rings, 12

NOTE: The most important thing when selecting bead colors is that you will enjoy looking at them—they do not need to exactly match the colors I used.

TECHNIQUES

Flat right angle weave

Tubular one-drop even-count peyote

Building tubular peyote from right angle weave

Embellishing right angle weave

Closed jump rings

Toggle clasp

Jump rings

FINISHED LENGTH

32 inches (81 cm)

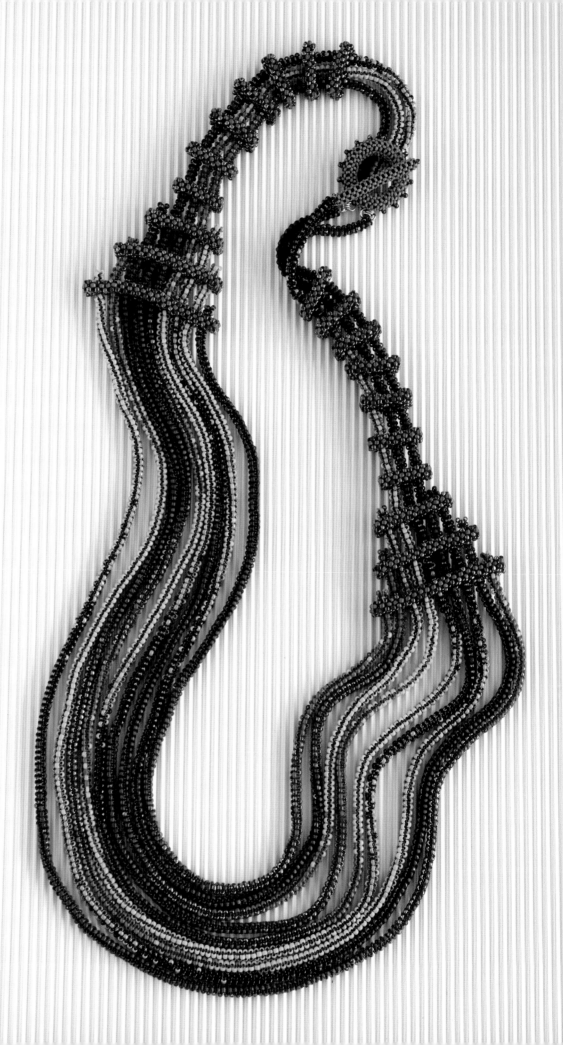

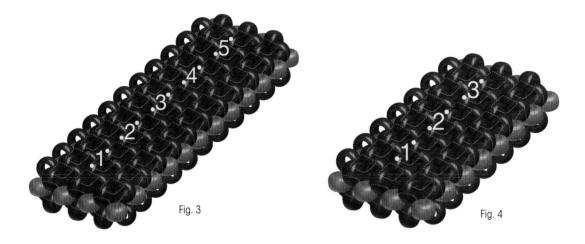

Fig. 3

Fig. 4

PEYOTE LENGTHS

Make nine tubular one-drop even-count peyote pieces in graduated lengths. Each subsequent length is 1 inch (2.5 cm) longer than the previous length, beginning with length 1 at 17 inches (43.2 cm). Work the peyote tube gradation freely from one color to the next in this order: A, B, C, D, E, F, G, H, and I. There is no pattern for the color gradation. Begin again at A and repeat until you reach the desired length. Try beginning with colors other than A or in the middle of a gradation. To gradate from one color to the next, add more rows of the next color until you make a number of rows in the new color. Repeat to gradate into the next color.

Length 1 is 17 inches (43.2 cm) long.
Length 2 is 18 inches (45.7 cm) long.
Length 3 is 19 inches (48.3 cm) long.
Length 4 is 20 inches (50.8 cm) long.
Length 5 is 21 inches (53.3 cm) long.
Length 6 is 22 inches (55.9 cm) long.
Length 7 is 23 inches (58.4 cm) long.
Length 8 is 24 inches (61 cm) long.
Length 9 is 25 inches (63.5 cm) long.

CONNECTING

Always use the yellow dot beads as the connection points for all the peyote lenghts. Add a nub after adding each length to a cuboid—weave through the cuboid and add four rows of tubular one-drop even-count peyote, continuing the bead color gradation. Nubs are added from the yellow dot beads on the side opposite from the lengths. Remember principle 3 of this type of tubular peyote: Allow the lengths to twist, and only then secure the length to the cuboid.

Length 1

Stitch the first two beads of the length to cuboid 1 at the first position. Weave through the cuboid and add a nub.

Stitch the last two beads of the length to cuboid 2 at the first position. Weave through the cuboid and add a nub.

Length 2

Stitch the first two beads of the length to cuboid 1 at the second position. Weave through the cuboid and add

nine rows of tubular peyote. Stitch the last two beads of the tube to cuboid 3 at the first position. Weave through the cuboid and add a nub.

Stitch the last two beads of the length to cuboid 2 at the second position. Weave through the cuboid and add nine rows of tubular peyote. Stitch the last two beads of the tube to cuboid 4 at the seventh position. Weave through the cuboid and add a nub.

Length 3

Stitch the first two beads of the length to cuboid 1 at the third position. Weave through the cuboid and add nine rows of tubular peyote. Stitch the last two beads added to cuboid 3 at the second position. Weave through the cuboid and add nine rows of tubular peyote. Stitch the last two beads of the tube to cuboid 5 at the first position. Weave through the cuboid and add a nub.

Stitch the last two beads of the length to cuboid 2 at the seventh position. Weave through the cuboid and add nine rows of tubular peyote. Stitch the last two beads of the tube to cuboid 4 at the sixth position. Weave through the cuboid and add nine rows of tubular peyote. Stitch the last two beads of the tube to cuboid 6 at the fifth position. Weave through the cuboid and add a nub.

Length 4

Stitch the first two beads of the length to cuboid 1 at the fourth position. Weave through the cuboid and add nine rows of tubular peyote. Stitch the last two beads of the tube to cuboid 3 at the third position. Weave through the cuboid and add nine rows of tubular peyote. Stitch the last two beads of the tube to cuboid 7 at the second position. Weave through the cuboid and add nine rows of tubular peyote. Repeat to add cuboids 9, 11, and 13. Weave through the cuboid and add five rows of tubular peyote. Stitch the last two beads of the tube to cuboid 15. Add five more rows of tubular peyote, and attach the last two rows to cuboid 17. Repeat, adding another five rows of tubular peyote and connecting cuboid 19. Weave through cuboid 19 and add 41 rows of tubular peyote. Stitch a closed jump ring to the last two beads.

Stitch the last two beads of the length to cuboid 2 at the sixth position. Weave through the cuboid and add nine rows of tubular peyote. Stitch the last two beads of the tube to cuboid 4 at the fifth position. Weave through the cuboid and add nine rows of tubular peyote. Stitch the last two beads of the tube to cuboid 6 at the fourth position. Weave through the cuboid and add nine rows of tubular peyote. Stitch the last two beads of the tube to cuboid 8 at the third position. Repeat to add cuboids 10, 12, and 14. Weave through the cuboid and add five rows of tubular peyote. Stitch the last two beads of the tube to cuboid 16. Add five more rows of tubular peyote and attach the last two rows to cuboid 18. Repeat, adding another five rows of tubular peyote and connecting cuboid 20. Weave through cuboid 20 and add 49 rows of tubular peyote. Stitch a closed jump ring to the last two beads.

Length 5

Stitch the first two beads of the length to cuboid 1 at the fifth position. Weave through the cuboid and add nine rows of tubular peyote. Stitch the last two beads of the tube to cuboid 3 at the fourth position. Weave through the cuboid and add nine rows of tubular peyote. Stitch the last two beads of the tube to cuboid 5 at the third position. Weave through the cuboid and add nine rows of tubular peyote. Stitch the last two beads of the tube to cuboid 7 at the second position. Repeat to add cuboids 9, 11, and 13. Weave through the cuboid and add seven rows of tubular peyote. Stitch the last two beads of the tube to cuboid 15. Add seven more rows of tubular peyote and attach the last two rows to cuboid 17. Repeat, adding another seven rows of tubular peyote and connecting cuboid 19. Weave through cuboid 19 and add 46 rows of tubular peyote. Stitch a closed jump ring to the last two beads.

Stitch the last two beads of the length to cuboid 2 at the fifth position. Weave through the cuboid and add nine rows of tubular peyote. Stitch the last two beads of the tube to cuboid 4 at the fourth position. Weave through the cuboid and add nine rows of tubular peyote. Stitch the last two beads of the tube to cuboid 6 at the third position. Weave through the cuboid and add nine rows of tubular peyote. Stitch the last two beads of the tube to cuboid 8 at the second position. Repeat to add cuboids 10, 12, and 14. Weave through the cuboid and add five rows of tubular peyote. Stitch the last two beads of the tube to cuboid 16. Add five more rows of tubular peyote, and attach the last two rows to cuboid 18. Repeat, adding another five rows of tubular peyote and connecting cuboid 20. Weave through cuboid 20 and add 54 rows of tubular peyote. Stitch a closed jump ring to the last two beads.

Length 6

Stitch the first two beads of the length to cuboid 1 at the sixth position. Weave through the cuboid and add nine rows of tubular peyote. Stitch the last two beads of the tube to cuboid 3 at the fifth position. Weave through the cuboid and add nine rows of tubular peyote. Stitch the last two beads of the tube to cuboid 5 at the fourth position. Weave through the cuboid and add nine rows of tubular peyote. Stitch the last two beads of the tube to cuboid 7 at the third position. Repeat to add cuboids 9, 11, 13, 15, 17, and 19 with nine rows of tubular peyote between each one. Weave through cuboid 19 and add 50 rows of tubular peyote. Stitch a closed jump ring to the last two beads.

Stitch the last two beads of the length to cuboid 2 at the fourth position. Weave through the cuboid and add nine rows of tubular peyote. Stitch the last two beads of the tube to cuboid 4 at the third position. Weave through the cuboid and add nine rows of tubular peyote. Stitch the last two beads of the tube to cuboid 6 at the second position. Weave through the cuboid and add nine rows of tubular peyote. Stitch the last two beads of the tube to cuboid 8 at the first position. Repeat to add cuboids 10, 12, 14, 16, 18, and 20 with nine rows of tubular peyote between each one. Weave through cuboid 20 and add 58 rows of tubular peyote. Stitch a closed jump ring to the last two beads.

Length 7

Stitch the first two beads of the length to cuboid 1 at the seventh position. Weave through the cuboid and add nine rows of tubular peyote. Stitch the last two beads of the tube to cuboid 3 at the sixth position. Weave through the cuboid and add nine rows of tubular peyote. Stitch the last two beads of the tube to cuboid 5 at the fifth position. Weave through the cuboid and add a nub.

Stitch the last two beads of the length to cuboid 2 at the third position. Weave through the cuboid and add nine rows of tubular peyote. Stitch the last two beads of the tube to cuboid 4 at the second position. Weave through the cuboid and add nine rows of tubular peyote. Stitch the last two beads of the tube to cuboid 6 at the first position. Weave through the cuboid and add a nub.

Length 8

Stitch the first two beads of the length to cuboid 1 at the eighth position. Weave through the cuboid and add nine rows of tubular peyote. Stitch the last two beads of the tube to cuboid 3 at the seventh position. Weave through the cuboid and add a nub.

Stitch the last two beads of the length to cuboid 2 at the second position. Weave through the cuboid and add nine rows of tubular peyote. Stitch the last two beads of the tube to cuboid 4 at the first position. Weave through the cuboid and add a nub.

Length 9

Stitch the first two beads of the length to cuboid 1 at the ninth position. Weave through the cuboid and add a nub.

Stitch the last two beads of the length to cuboid 2 at the first position. Weave through the cuboid and add a nub.

CLOSURE

Make the loop by covering a 1-inch (2.5 cm) plastic ring with 15°s in a strip of one-drop right angle weave 31 units long and six units wide. Close the length into a loop with a 32nd row and the width into a tube with a seventh row. Stitch three closed jump rings one unit apart, and embellish every other unit of the same row with one A. Connect the closed jump rings on the loop to the closed jump rings at the ends of lengths 4, 5, and 6 with two jump rings each.

Make the bar by covering a 1¼-inch (3.2 cm) length of 16-gauge round wire with a strip of one-drop right angle weave 15 units long and four units wide. Close the length into a tube with a fifth row. Cinch the ends and embellish with As. Stitch three closed jump rings to the middle of the bar spaced with one unit between each of them. Connect the closed jump rings on the bar to the closed jump rings at the second ends of lengths 4, 5, and 6 with two jump rings each.

Chapter 2

EARRINGS

B'ALEXANDER EARRINGS

Darius B'Alexander is a maker of many objects strange and wonderful—among them are cut paper critters he posts to Facebook that inspired this project. I met him twenty years ago when I was working at my first bead shop at Bead It in Santa Cruz, California.

OVERVIEW

Tubular peyote with peyote beads waggle and extend like make-believe monster arms from a right angle ring. Top the ring with a wave of beadwork and finish the earring with ear wires.

RIGHT ANGLE WEAVE RING

Make two rings and set them aside.

Make a right angle weave ring as specified in "Fundamentals" that begins with 16×3 units of 11's and 15's in the first step, and follows exactly the second and third steps.

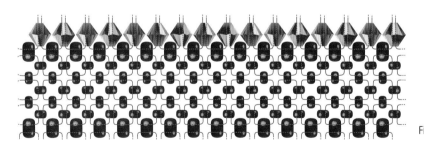

Fig. 1

WAVE AND APPENDAGES

Make a wave component that sits atop a right angle weave ring for a fanciful little finish. Five arm- and leg-like tubular peyote and peyote bead appendages extend from five right angle weave ring positions. Finish each appendage with a crystal and 15° embellishment.

Use 11's to stitch a base of modified right angle weave. See figure 2.

NOTE: It is called modified because there are three rather than four sides to each unit. Make a second base.

Fig. 2

SUPPLIES

Beadweaving kit

11° round opaque red AB seed beads, 4 grams

15° round transparent red matte AB seed beads, <1 gram

3mm hyacinth 2XAB bicone crystal beads, 42

4mm silver closed jump rings, 2

Silver ear wires

Red thread

TECHNIQUES

Right angle weave ring

Tubular one-drop even-count peyote

Peyote bead

Peyote bead embellishment

Building tubular peyote from right angle weave

Wavy chain

Closed jump ring

Ear wires

FINISHED LENGTH

3 inches (7.6 cm)

Continue in right angle weave to bind the edges with 11°s (blue line). See figure 3.

NOTE: You can attach the closed jump ring and ear wire now, but it will snag your working thread as you execute the remainder of the project.

Bind the wave to the ring, stitching two sets of 11°s on the front and back of the wave to two crystals of the ring and repeat to bind at the second point (blue lines). See figure 4.

Weave to position 1. Starting from the two crystals, add 14 rows of tubular peyote, a peyote bead, and the embellishment. Repeat four more times, adding 24 rows of peyote and a peyote bead to positions 2 and 4, and 14 rows of peyote and a peyote bead to positions 3 and 5.

FINISHING

Stitch a closed jump ring to the wave using the left and right beads of the center unit. Attach the ear wire loop to the closed jump ring. Repeat to finish the second earring. See figure 5.

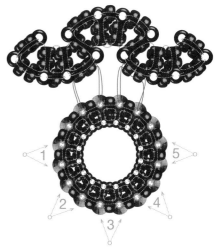

Fig. 3

Fig. 4

Fig. 5

GOOD LIZ EARRINGS

SUPPLIES

Beadweaving kit

Size 11° round seed
beads:
   A, matte aqua,
      2 grams
   B, matte olive,
      <1 gram
   C, matte fuchsia,
      <1 gram
   D, bronze
      metallic, 1 gram

Size 15° bronze
   metallic round
   seed beads,
   <1 gram

4mm gold closed
   jump rings, 2

Gold lever-back ear
   wires

Gold thread

Chain-nose pliers

TECHNIQUES

Cuboids

Right angle weave

Tubular peyote

Peyote bead

Ear wires

FINISHED
LENGTH

2 ⅜ inches (6 cm)

Three Vs in a row attached with peyote. Add more chevrons; they've got room to grow. These babies are named after my first great teaching assistant and most inquisitive student, Liz Penn.

OVERVIEW

Add a peyote bead to three V-shaped cuboids connected with tubular peyote.

COMPONENTS

Use right angle weave to make two faces of each color with a 90° bend at the middle. Bind the two faces in the manner used to make a cuboid (red line in the right column of figure 1). Make the large nine-unit component with aqua seed beads. Make the medium seven-unit component with olive seed beads. Make the small five-unit component with fuchsia seed beads. Stitch a 3mm crystal and 15° anchor bead to both ends of each component (blue line).

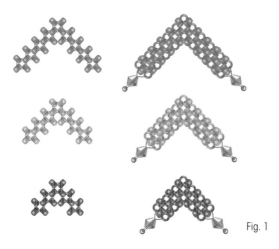

Fig. 1

FINISHING

Begin at the top of the earring and work toward the bottom, joining components together as you go. Remember to reinforce each round of tubular peyote.

Fig. 2

RING, RED LINE

Exit the thread from the topmost A. String four 15°s and the jump ring, then pass through the topmost A again. Reinforce with two or more passes.

JOIN 1, BLUE LINE

Exit the thread from the left inside binding bead of the larger component. String a D, pass through the right inside binding bead, string a D, and pass through the left inside binding bead again. Step up through the first D added. Continue in tubular peyote to add two rounds of D and step up.

JOIN 2, GREEN AND BLACK LINES

Stitch through the front D and four beads in right angle weave of the next component (Bs when adding the medium component and Cs when adding the small component) and stitch through the D again. Repeat to tighten the back D to the right angle weave unit on the back of the component.

Repeat joins 1 and 2 to attach the small component.

BEAD AND EMBELLISHMENT, GOLD LINE

Build a peyote bead of Ds beginning at round 3. Stitch a 3mm crystal and a 15° anchor bead to the cinch round.

Attach the ear wire to the closed jump ring.

Repeat to make the second earring.

NARTRI EARRINGS

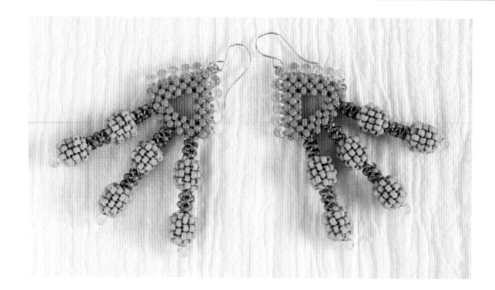

My favorite bead is featured in these earrings—the discontinued ancient green bead made by Toho. The design is a take on traditional brick stitch earrings, which would begin with a triangle of beadwork and flow into a multitude of fringe.

OVERVIEW

A right angle weave triangle supports three drops of tubular peyote and peyote beads. Embellish the triangle with drop beads, and finish it with a bead loop, a closed jump ring, and an ear wire.

Use A in right angle weave to stitch and bind two triangular faces.

Fig. 1

FRINGE

Tubular peyote and peyote bead fringe extend from three positions on the triangle bottom. Finish each with a drop bead. See figure 2.

Stitch five rows of tubular peyote with B and two rows with C. Build a peyote bead in C from the last two rows just added. Stitch five rows of tubular peyote with B, and two rows with C starting from the final row of the peyote bead. Build a peyote bead in C from the last two rows just added. Add a drop bead embellishment. Repeat to add the same fringe at all three positions.

Fig. 2

Beadweaving kit

11° round seed beads:
  A, opaque bright orange, 2 grams
  B, transparent olivine gold frost, 1 gram
  C, opaque olivine matte, 5 grams

15° round opaque bright orange seed beads, <1 gram

3.4mm transparent olivine drop seed beads, 26

4mm sterling silver 20-gauge closed jump rings, 2

Sterling silver ear wires

Gold thread

TECHNIQUES

Tubular one-drop even-count peyote

Peyote bead

Peyote bead embellishment

Building tubular peyote from right angle weave

Closed jump ring

Ear wires

FINISHED LENGTH

2¾ inches (7 cm)

FINISHING

Embellish five top open units of the triangle with drop seed beads. Repeat on the other side of the triangle. See figure 3.

Exit the topmost triangle bead and string six 15°s and a closed jump ring. Stitch through the top triangle bead again in a circle. Stitch through all to reinforce.

Attach an ear wire. Repeat to make the second earring.

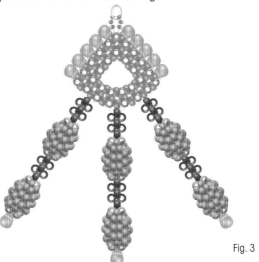

Fig. 3

SEUSSICAL EARRINGS

These remind me of some sort of fantastical tree from a Dr. Seuss book—but for your ears.

OVERVIEW

Use drop seed beads rather than round seed beads to bind cuboid faces. Join the cuboids with tubular peyote and finish the bottoms with a simple embellishment and the tops with lever-back ear wires.

CUBOIDS

Make 24 three-by-three-unit right angle weave faces with As. Use right angle weave to bind the two faces together using 3.4mm drop seed beads. Bind the yellow dot beads of the top face to the corresponding beads on the bottom face as in figure 14 on page 15. (See figure 1.).

Fig. 1

SUPPLIES

Beadweaving kit

Size 11° round seed beads:
  A, matte fuchsia, 5 grams
  B, matte chartreuse, 1 gram

Size 15° matte chartreuse seed beads, 2

3.4mm transparent red drop seed beads, 144

8×5mm chartreuse faceted glass rondelle, 2

7×4mm chartreuse faceted glass rondelle, 2

3mm jet 2XAB bicone crystal, 2

Sterling silver lever-back ear wires

Red thread

Chain-nose pliers

TECHNIQUES

Cuboids

Tubular peyote

Ear wires

FINISHED LENGTH

3½ inches (8.9 cm)

FINISHING

Referring to figure 2, work from the bottom to the top, beginning with the sixth cuboid. Weave a thread into the bottom cuboid to exit the first blue dot A. String a large rondelle, a small rondelle, a 3mm crystal, and a 15°. Stitch back through the 3mm crystal and both rondelles, and then stitch through the blue dot A opposite from the first. Reinforce this thread path until the embellishment beads are secure. *Exit the thread through the top of the cuboid and build four rounds of tubular peyote in B from the yellow dot As, stitching the fourth row to the blue dot As on the bottom of the next cuboid. Repeat from * to incorporate the fourth, third, second, and first cuboids. Build one more four-round peyote tube onto the yellow dot As on the topmost cuboid. Stitch a closed jump ring to the Bs in the fourth row. Attach the lever-back loop to the jump ring.

Repeat to make the second earring.

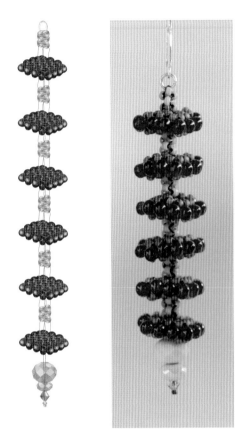

Fig. 2

TUPOD EARRINGS

SUPPLIES

Beadweaving kit

Size 11° opaque turquoise round seed beads, 4 grams

Size 15° round seed beads:
A, opaque turquoise, 1 gram
B, gold metallic, 1 gram
C, silver-lined red AB, 1 gram

Gold ear wires

Gold thread

Chain-nose pliers

TECHNIQUES

Right angle weave

Tubular peyote

Ear wires

FINISHED LENGTH

2 inches (5 cm)

Lightweight pod earrings are beautiful all the way around. Making them is like sewing a jacket and lining it, too.

OVERVIEW

Build tubular peyote bumps up from a right angle weave base made in varying counts, embellished, and then closed into a tube. Rectangular openings of right angle weave are unembellished.

BASE

In right angle weave with a varying drop count, make a flat base. Please observe that beads are added on three sides of some units.

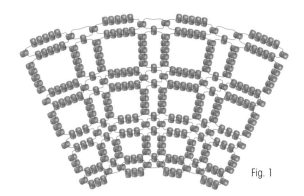

Fig. 1

SIDE BUMPS

Made in tubular even-count peyote, these bump patterns fill the right angle weave openings most visible when being worn. Round 1 of each bump is a transition from right angle weave to tubular even-count peyote. The final round of each bump is a cinch round—you'll pass through the last round of beads in a circular pattern and pull the thread taut. All bumps begin with 11°s and end with 15°s. Once you've completed a bump, weave through the beadwork to begin the next bump.

NOTE: Some of the thread paths in the illustrations appear loose, with a considerable amount of thread exposed. This is for illustration purposes only—you should add each round of beads in the bumps with a fair amount of tension.

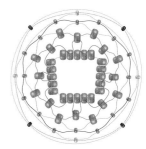

Fig. 2

Tall

This bump is worked on a right angle weave unit that has five beads on every side. See figure 2 for all rounds.

ROUND 1

Weave through the base to exit the second bead on any side of a five-drop unit. *String one 11° and pass through the fourth bead on the same side of the unit. String one 11° and pass through the second bead on the next side of the unit. Repeat from * three more times. Step up by passing though the first 11° added in the round (red line).

ROUND 2

String one 11° and pass through the next 11° in round 1. Repeat seven more times. Step up through the first 11° added in the round (blue line).

ROUND 3

String one A and pass through the next 11° in round 2. Repeat seven more times. Step up through the first A added in the round (green line).

ROUND 4

String one A and pass through the next A in round 3. Repeat seven more times. Step up through the first A added in the round (black line).

ROUND 5

String one B and pass through the next two As in round 4. Repeat three more times. Step up through the first B added in the round (gold line).

ROUND 6

String one C and pass through the next B in round 5. Repeat three more times. Step up through the first C added in the round (purple line).

CINCH

Pass two times through the last four Bs twice to form a circle (rose line) and pull taut.

Medium

This bump is worked on a right angle weave unit that has five beads on the top side, four beads on the left and right sides, and three beads on the bottom side. See figure 3 for all rounds.

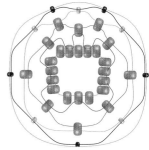

Fig. 3

ROUND 1

Weave through the beads to exit the fourth base bead of the five-drop side of the unit in a clockwise direction. String one 11° and pass through the second and third base beads of the next (four-drop) side. String one 11° and pass through the middle bead of the next (three-drop) side. String one 11° and pass through the second and third base beads of the next (four-drop) side. String one 11° and pass through the second bead on the next (five-drop) side. String one 11° and pass through the fourth bead on the same side. Step up at the end of the round by passing through the first beaded added (red line).

ROUND 2

String one 11° and pass through the next 11° in round 1. Repeat four more times. Step up through the first bead added (blue line).

ROUND 3

String one B and pass through the next 11° in round 2. Repeat four more times. Step up through the first bead added (green line).

ROUND 4

String one C and pass through the next B in round 3. Repeat four more times. Step up through the first bead added (black line).

CINCH

Pass two times through the last five Cs to form a circle (gold line) and pull taut.

Small

This bump is worked on a right angle weave unit that has three beads on every side. See figure 4 for all rounds.

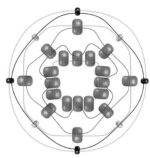

Fig. 4

ROUND 1

Weave through the base to exit the second base bead on any side. String one 11° and pass through the second base bead on the next side of the same unit. Repeat three more times. Step up at the end of the round by passing through the first 11° added (red line).

ROUND 2

String one 11° and pass through the next 11° in round 1. Repeat three more times. Step up through the first bead added (blue line).

ROUND 3

String one B and pass through the next 11° in round 2. Repeat three more times. Step up through the first bead added (green line).

ROUND 4

String one C and pass through the next B in round 3. Repeat three more times. Step up through the first bead added (black line).

CINCH

Pass two times through the last four Cs added to form a circle (gold line) and pull taut.

TUBE

Close the embellished flat right angle weave by stitching the first units to the last units, adding six red dot 11°s to continue the base pattern (red line).

TOP AND BOTTOM BUMPS

Less visible, but nonetheless important, these bumps finish off the pod. Refer to figure 5.

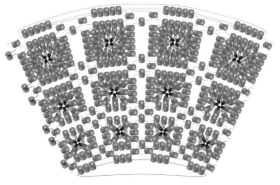

Fig. 5

Cinch the four sets of three 11°s to form a circle (blue line) and fill the unit with a small bump. Cinch the four sets of five 11°s to form a circle (green line) and fill the unit with a large bump.

FINISHING
Stitch a six-bead loop of As to two opposing As of the top bump. Add an ear wire to the loop. Repeat to finish the second earring.

TWINKLE DROP EARRINGS

This fun, sparkling earring matches up nicely to the Marseeah necklace.

SUPPLIES

Beadweaving kit

11° chartreuse matte round seed beads, 2 grams

15° chartreuse matte round seed beads, <1 gram

3.4mm gold-lined aqua drop seed beads, 8

12mm crystal AB rivoli chaton, 2

8.5×17mm fuchsia #6010 pendant, 2

Silver lever-back ear wires

Gold thread

Chain-nose pliers

TECHNIQUES

Twinkle drop

Ear wires

FINISHED LENGTH

2 inches (5 cm)

OVERVIEW

Make two twinkle drops and turn them into earrings by adding a simple bead loop and lever-back ear wires.

MAKE A TWINKLE DROP

Add and reinforce a four-bead loop of 15°s to the 11° on the bezel at position 8 (refer to figure 22 on page 19). Attach a lever-back ear wire to the bead loop.

Repeat to make a second earring.

QUATTUOR EARRINGS

SUPPLIES

Beadweaving kit

Size 11° round seed
  beads:
  A, opaque
    turquoise, 2
    grams
  B, gold metallic,
    <1 gram

Size 15° round gold
  metallic seed
  beads, 2 grams

3mm jet 2XAB
  bicone crystals, 48

Gold ear wires

Gold thread

TECHNIQUES

Right angle weave
  ring

Tubular peyote

Ear wires

FINISHED
LENGTH

2 inches (5 cm)

Sparkling components form gorgeous earrings named for the Proto-Indo term for "four." Gold beads seal the deal.

OVERVIEW

Make right angle weave rings. Link the rings together with tubular peyote. Add a bead loop at the top and attach ear wires.

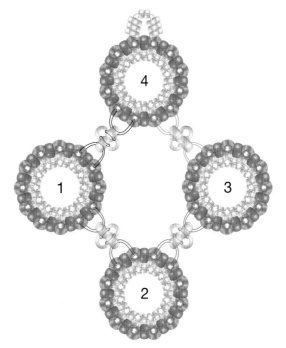

RINGS

For each earring, make four right angle weave rings with 15°s, As, and crystals. Stitch the initial strip 11 units long, and close it into a loop with a 12th unit. Fold the edges together, and bind the edges with 12 3mm crystals.

ATTACHING

Incorporate four right angle weave rings to create the main component for each earring.

RED LINE

Build three rows of tubular peyote in B up from two adjacent crystals of ring 1. Continue in tubular peyote, and attach the last row of peyote to two crystals of ring 2.

BLUE LINE

Weave through ring 2 and build three rows of tubular peyote up from the next set of two crystals. Continue in tubular peyote, and attach the last row of peyote to two crystals of ring 3.

GREEN LINE

Weave through ring 3 and build three rows of tubular peyote up from a set of two crystals. Continue in tubular peyote, and attach the last row of peyote to two crystals of ring 4.

BLACK LINE

Weave through ring 4 and build three rows of tubular peyote up from a set of two crystals. Continue in tubular peyote, and attach the last row of peyote to two crystals of ring 1.

FINISHING

Identify the two top crystals of ring 4. Exit the thread forward through the left crystal, string eight 15°s, pass to the back through the right crystal, string three 15°s, pass in the opposite direction through the fourth and fifth 15°s just added, string three 15°s, and pass forward through the left crystal again. Repeat the thread path to secure.

Use chain-nose pliers to attach an ear wire to the bead loop.

Repeat to finish the second earring.

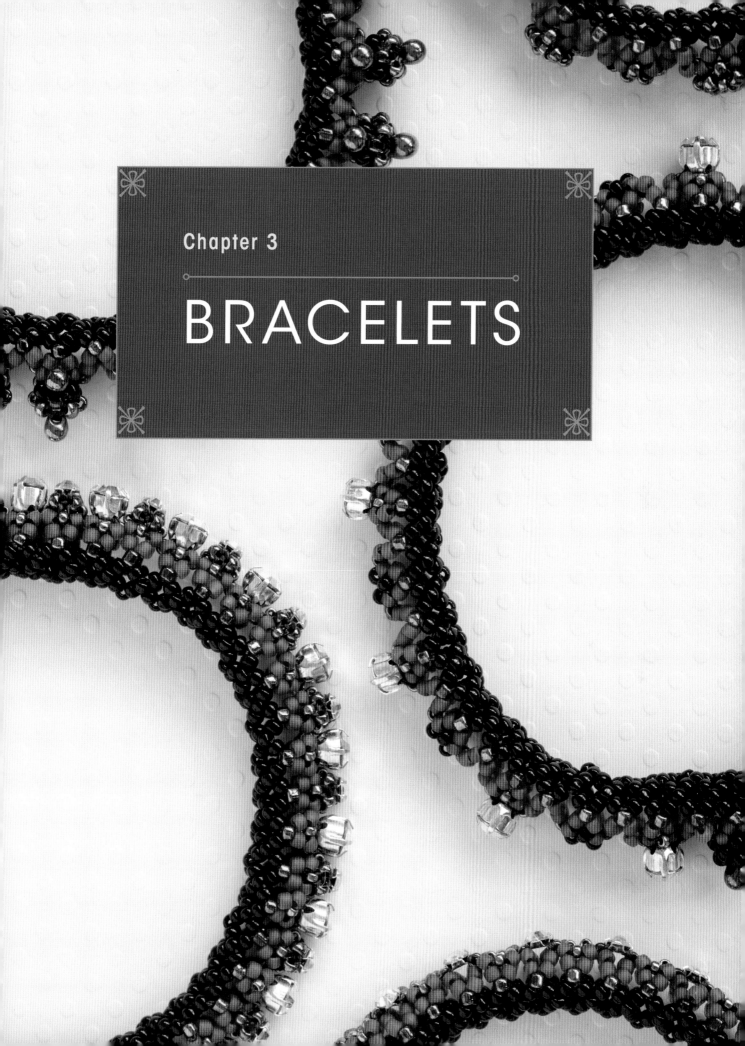

Chapter 3

BRACELETS

BARABEDES BRACELET

Undulated steps are linked into a graphic bracelet with a bright personality.

OVERVIEW

Make colorful cubic right angle weave bars and connect them with black and white beads in tubular peyote. Make a double-strand hook-and-loop closure with right angle weave and tubular peyote.

Cuboids

Each cuboid is one unit wide and one unit deep, and made using right angle weave and a single thread. Complete the bars and set them aside.

CUBOID 1

Stitch two strips of right angle weave nine units long and one unit wide with A. Align the strips and continue in right angle weave to bind the edges with A. Make five.

CUBOID 2

Stitch two strips of right angle weave 11 units long and one unit wide with B. Align the strips and continue in right angle wave to bind the edges with B. Make six.

CUBOID 3

Stitch two strips of right angle weave 13 units long and one unit wide with C. Align the strips and continue in right angle weave to bind the edges with C. Make six.

CUBOID 4

Stitch two strips of right angle weave 13 units long and one unit wide with B. Align the strips and continue in right angle weave to bind the edges with B. Make three.

CUBOID 5

Stitch two strips of right angle weave nine units long and one unit wide with D. Align the strips and continue in right angle weave to bind the edges with D. Make two.

Positions

The cuboids will be connected with tubular peyote in a way and with specific colors that will make the connections appear continuous—but they are not. One unit separates all adjacent positions.

CUBOID 1

The first position is at the first unit of the cuboid.

CUBOID 2

The first position is at the second unit of the cuboid.

CUBOIDS 3 AND 4

The first position is at the third unit of the cuboid.

CUBOID 5

The first position is at the first unit of the cuboid.

SUPPLIES

Beadweaving kit

11° round seed beads:
- A, opaque bright orange, 6 grams
- B, translucent matte fuchsia, 8 grams
- C, opaque red AB, 6 grams
- D, orange-lined transparent topaz AB, 2 grams
- E, opaque black, 4 grams
- F, opaque white, 3 grams

15° round bright orange seed beads, <1 gram

Red thread

TECHNIQUES

Cuboids

Tubular one-drop even-count peyote

Building tubular peyote from right angle weave

FINISHED LENGTH

7½ inches (19 cm)

Connecting

Work connections up from the prescribed position on the cuboid. All connections are three rows of tubular peyote. Use E to create all connections at positions 1, 3, and 5. Use F to create all connections at positions 2 and 4.

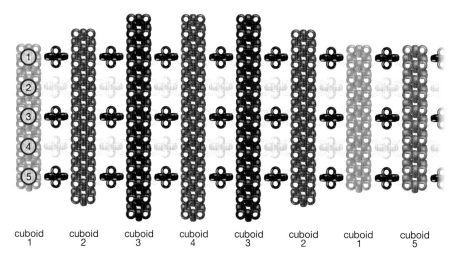

cuboid 1 cuboid 2 cuboid 3 cuboid 4 cuboid 3 cuboid 2 cuboid 1 cuboid 5

Fig. 1

Note: It is easier to add all connections to a cuboid and then attach them all to the next cuboid. It is cumbersome to create a connection, attach it to the next cuboid, create the second connection, attach it to the next cuboid, and so on. While adding subsequent connections, the thread will readily snap on the beadwork.

1

Begin with a cuboid 1. Add connections at positions 1–5. Stitch the last beads of each connection to the corresponding positions 1–5 of a cuboid 2.

2

Add connections to positions 1–5 of a cuboid 2, then stitch the last beads of each connection to the corresponding position 1–5 of a cuboid 3.

3

Continue in this manner to connect the remaining cuboids in this order: 4, 3, 2, 1, 5, 1, 2, 3, 4, 3, 2, 1, 5, 1, 2, 3, 4, 3, and 2.

4

Add connections to a cuboid 2.

Hook-and-Loop Clasp

This clasp integrates right into the bracelet concept as you make it with the same stitches as the cuboids. It would work made in E or F, too.

LOOP

While this half of the clasp is not literally a loop, it serves the purpose of a loop.

Stitch a flat piece of A in right angle weave nine units tall and four units wide with two openings. See Figure 2. Make a second piece.

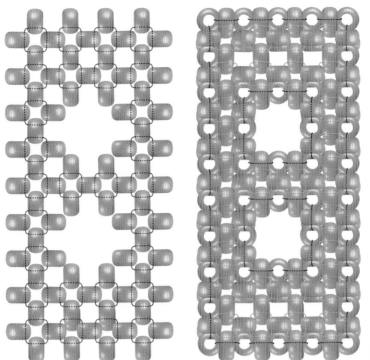

Fig. 2

Fig. 3

Align the pieces and continue in right angle weave to bind all outer and inner edges (red line). See figure 3.

Stitch it to the five connections added to the final cuboid 2.

HOOK

Work 27 rows of 11°s and 15°s in tubular peyote up from the last cuboid 1 at positions 2 and 4 to add two hooks. See figure 4. Weave thread to position 2.

ROUNDS 1–8

Add two As in each round.

ROUND 9

Add one A and one 15°.

ROUND 10

Add two As in each round.

Fig. 4

ROUNDS 11–27

Repeat rounds 9 and 10, finishing with a round 9 repeat.

Stitch one A to the round 27 beads to finish off the end of the repeat from round 1 to add a second hook at position 4.

BIENENBAUS BRACELET

SUPPLIES

Beadweaving kit

Size 8° opaque olive
round seed beads,
<1 gram

Size 11° round seed
beads:
  A, opaque orange,
    12 grams
  B, opaque olive,
    7 grams
  C, silver-lined
    chartreuse,
    3 grams

Size 15° matte olive
round seed beads,
<1 gram

Gold thread

TECHNIQUES

Cuboids

Right angle weave

Tubular peyote

Right angle weave
ring

Peyote bead

FINISHED
LENGTH

8 inches (20 cm)

This multistrand bracelet is made of bright orange and olive beads for a fun contrast. The peyote beads and peyote lengths complement one another from one strand to the next, undulating in and out, giving this project its name.

OVERVIEW

Connect two cuboids with tubular peyote lengths interspersed with peyote beads. Add four-row extensions to the cuboids and finish up with a right angle ring and peyote bead clasp.

CUBOIDS

Stitch a cuboid 11 units long and three units wide. Make the faces with orange beads and bind the edges with olive beads. Bind the corresponding beads of the front and back faces together where indicated with red, blue, green, black, and purple dots.

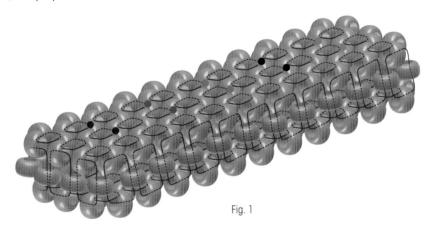

Fig. 1

PEYOTE LENGTHS

Build lengths of tubular peyote in olive and silver-lined chartreuse beads starting from the cuboids made in one-drop right angle weave. The tubular peyote extends between peyote beads made of olive and orange beads. The one-drop tube increases into a peyote bead, and then decreases back to one-drop for a count of rows. Each peyote length extends from matched sets of corresponding dots. Each length of peyote and peyote beads extends from the red set of dots of the first cuboid to the set of red dots on the second cuboid until five lengths of peyote connect the two cuboids. Note how rounds 1 and 2 of the peyote bead are added in contrast with how round 10 is added while appearing to be symmetrical. When completing a length, weave thread in or pass through a cuboid to exit the other side and begin the clasp and finishing step. Remember to reinforce everything with a second pass.

NOTE: Rounds 17 and 18 represent one round of the peyote bead, but two rounds of tubular peyote.

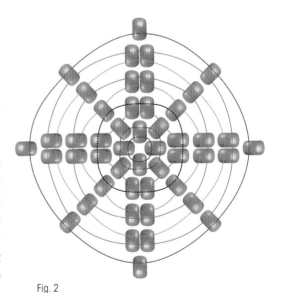

Fig. 2

Peyote bead pattern of As and Bs

Remember principle 3 of this type of tubular peyote: Allow the length to twist, and then secure the length to the cuboid—each length will rotate around approximately two times. See figure 2.

Red, Green, and Purple Lines (Figure 3)

Note: Line colors for each round refer to figure 2 on page 83.

TUBULAR ROUND 1
Add two Cs to the As indicated with dots.

TUBULAR ROUND 2
Add two Cs.

TUBULAR ROUNDS 3–5
Add two Bs in each round.

TUBULAR ROUNDS 6–7
Add two Cs in each round.

TUBULAR ROUNDS 8–9 AND BEAD ROUNDS 1–2, RED LINE
Add two As in each round.

TUBULAR ROUND 10 AND BEAD ROUND 3, BLUE LINE
Increase by adding four Bs, one at a time, between the As added in the previous two rounds.

TUBULAR ROUND 11 AND BEAD ROUND 4, GREEN LINE
Increase by adding eight As, two at a time, between the Bs added in the previous round.

TUBULAR ROUND 12 AND BEAD ROUND 5, BLACK LINE
Add four Bs one at a time.

TUBULAR ROUND 13 AND BEAD ROUND 6, GOLD LINE
Add eight As two at a time.

TUBULAR ROUND 14 AND BEAD ROUND 7, PURPLE LINE
Add four Bs one at a time.

TUBULAR ROUND 15 AND BEAD ROUND 8, ROSE LINE
Add eight As two at a time.

TUBULAR ROUND 16 AND BEAD ROUND 9, AQUA LINE
Add four Bs one at a time.

TUBULAR ROUNDS 17–18 AND BEAD ROUND 10, BROWN LINE
Decrease by adding four As one at a time.

CINCH
Pass in a circle through the four As just added—do not include the beads from the previous round.

TUBULAR ROUND 19
Add Cs to two of the last four As just added.

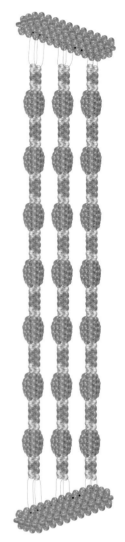

Fig. 3

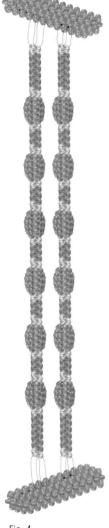

Fig. 4

TUBULAR ROUND 20
Add two Cs in each round.

TUBULAR ROUNDS 21–25
Add two Bs in each round.

CONTINUING
Repeat rounds 6–19 five more times.

FINISHING
Add three rounds of Bs and two rounds of Cs. Continue in tubular peyote to stitch the last two Cs added to the As on the second cuboid marked with the corresponding dot color.

Blue and Black Lines (Figure 4)
Note: Line colors for each round refer to figure 2 on page 83.

TUBULAR ROUND 1
Add two Cs to the As indicated with dots.

TUBULAR ROUND 2
Add Cs.

TUBULAR ROUNDS 3–13
Add Bs.

TUBULAR ROUNDS 14–15
Add Cs.

TUBULAR ROUNDS 16–17 AND BEAD ROUNDS 1–2, RED LINE
Add two As in each round.

TUBULAR ROUND 18 AND BEAD ROUND 3, BLUE LINE
Increase by adding four Bs one at a time between the As added in the previous two rounds.

TUBULAR ROUND 19 AND BEAD ROUND 4, GREEN LINE
Increase by adding eight As two at a time.

TUBULAR ROUND 20 AND BEAD ROUND 5, BLACK LINE
Add four Bs one at a time.

TUBULAR ROUND 21 AND BEAD ROUND 6, GOLD LINE
Add eight As two at a time.

TUBULAR ROUND 22 AND BEAD ROUND 7, PURPLE LINE
Add four Bs one at a time.

TUBULAR ROUND 23 AND BEAD ROUND 8, ROSE LINE
Add eight As two at a time.

TUBULAR ROUND 24 AND BEAD ROUND 9, AQUA LINE

Add four Bs one at a time.

TUBULAR ROUND 25 AND BEAD ROUND 10, BROWN LINE

Add four As one at a time.

CINCH

Pass in a circle through the four As just added—do not include beads from the previous round.

TUBULAR ROUND 26

Add Cs to two of the last four As just added.

TUBULAR ROUND 27

Add two Cs in each round.

TUBULAR ROUNDS 28–32

Add two Bs in each round.

CONTINUING

Repeat rounds 14–27 five more times.

FINISHING

Add 11 rounds of Bs and two rounds of Cs. Stitch the last two Cs added to the As on the cuboid indicated with the corresponding dot color.

CLASP AND FINISHING

Work one end at a time—begin with either. The round counts were set in such a way that when the clasp is closed, the ring appears to be centered between the opposing cuboids. Work on the side of cuboids opposite the peyote lengths. Add the clasp and finishing before or after the peyote lengths—it is up to you!

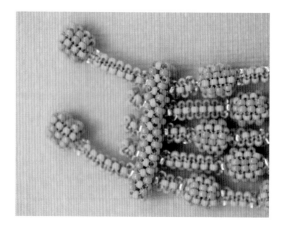

Both Ends

At the black, green, and blue dot sets, add five rounds of tubular peyote—two rounds of Cs, followed by three rounds of Bs.

Peyote Beads

Make a peyote bead as in figure 1 and attach with a 15-row length of tubular peyote. Repeat to add a second peyote bead in the same manner. Add three 4-bead extensions. See figure 5.

ROUND 1

Add two Cs to two of the last four As just cinched.

ROUND 2

Add two Cs.

ROUNDS 3–13

Add two Bs.

ROUNDS 14–15

Add two Cs.

FINISHING

Stitch the last two Cs added to the As on the cuboid indicated with the red dots.

Add a second peyote bead and peyote length to the purple dots.

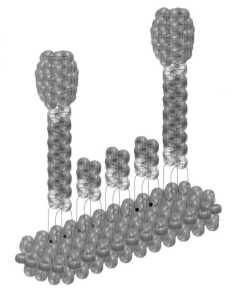

Fig. 5

Right Angle Weave Rings

Make two rings with a total of 13 units, and set one aside. Build a peyote length up from the cuboid at the red dots. See figure 6.

ROUND 1

Add two Cs to the red dot As on the cuboid indicated with red dots.

ROUND 2

Add two Cs.

ROUNDS 3–7

Add two Bs.

ROUNDS 8–9

Add two Cs.

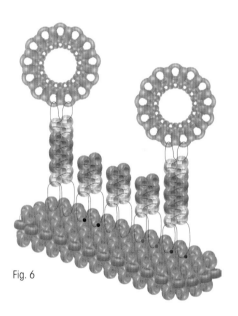

Fig. 6

FINISHING

Continuing in tubular peyote, stitch the last two Cs added to two 8°s on one of the rings.

Repeat to add a second peyote length and ring to the purple dots.

CUSTOM SIZES

Adjust the number of rounds of C added at either end of the lengths to adjust the overall bracelet length. Remember to repeat the pattern between the red, green, and purple lines as well as the blue and black lines.

BOROBUDUR BANGLES

Worked in tubular netting with embellishment variations and filled in with tubular peyote, this project was inspired by Indian architecture of a Buddhist temple in Central Java, Indonesia. My grandmother visited Borobudur and prayed for her first grandchild to be a girl.

OVERVIEW

Stitch lengths of tubular peyote and close them into bracelets. Then, fill openings in the netting with various embellishments.

ALL ABOUT THAT BASE

Create a tube of even-count netting. The number of beads added with each stitch varies from round to round. The point where each round begins rotates by one set of beads as the rounds progress. For every round, repeat the thread path without adding new beads. See figure 1.

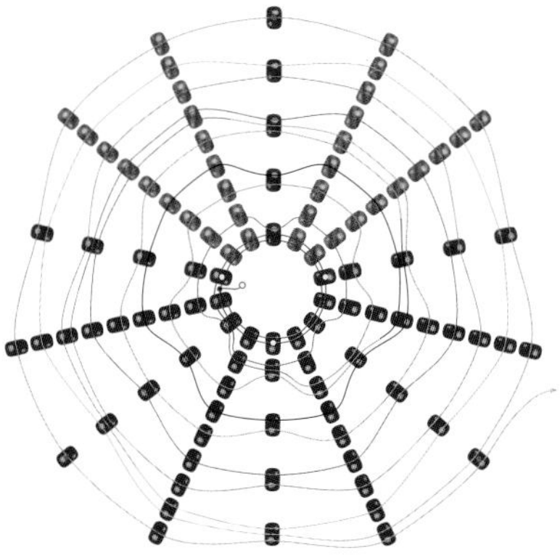

INITIAL RING, RED LINE

String seven As, one B, two Cs, one B, two Cs, and one B and stitch through the loop again. Tie a double overhand knot and stitch through the first two As again.

BLUE LINE

String three As and stitch through the sixth A of the initial ring. String one A, one B, and two Cs and stitch through the second B added in the initial ring. String two Cs, one B, and one A and stitch through the second A of the initial ring. Repeat the thread path without adding new beads. Step up through the two As first added to the round.

GREEN LINE

String three As and stitch through the first B added to the previous round, String two Cs, one B, and two Cs and stitch through the second B added to the previous round. String three As and stitch through the second A added to the previous round. Step up through the two As first added to the round.

BLACK LINE

String one A, one B, and two Cs and stitch through the first B added to the previous round. String two Cs, one B, and one A and stitch through the fifth A added to the previous round. String three As and stitch through the second A added to the previous round. Step up through the one A and one B first added to the round.

GOLD LINE

String two Cs, one B, and two Cs and stitch through the second B added to the previous round. String three As and stitch through the fourth A added to the previous round. String three As and stitch through the first B added to the previous round. Step up through the two Cs and one B first added in the round.

PURPLE LINE

String two Cs, one B, and one A and stitch through the second A added to previous round. String three As and stitch through the fifth A added to the previous round. String one A, one B, and two Cs and stitch through the B added to the previous round. Step up through the two Cs and one B first added to the round.

Fig. 1

SUPPLIES

Beadweaving kit

Size 11° round seed beads:
A, opaque black, 40 grams
B, ruby silver-lined AB, 5 grams
C, transparent matte fuchsia, 40 grams
D, dark silver metallic, 1 gram
E, bronze metallic, 1 gram

15° round dark silver metallic seed beads, 1 gram

3.4mm bronze metallic drop seed beads, 72

31ss crystal AB chaton montées, 36

16ss crystal AB rose montées, 48

Red thread

TECHNIQUES

Tubular one-drop even-count peyote

Peyote bead

Tubular netting

FINISHED LENGTH

Four bracelets that fit a 7- to 8-inch wrist

Fig. 2

ROSE LINE

String three As and stitch through the third A added to the previous round. String three As and stitch through the second B added to the previous round. String two Cs, one B, and two Cs and stitch through the first B added to the previous round. Step up through the two As first added to the round.

AQUA LINE

String three As and stitch through the fifth A added to the previous round. String one A, one B, and two Cs and stitch through the B added to the previous round. String two Cs, one B, and one A and stitch through the second A added to the previous round. Step up through the two As first added to the round.

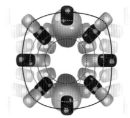

Fig. 3

BROWN LINE

String three As and stitch through the first B added to the previous round. String two Cs, one B, and two Cs and stitch through the second B added to the previous round. String three As and stitch through the second A added to the previous round. Step up through the two As first added to the round.

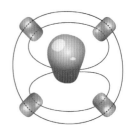

Fig. 4

FINISHING

Referring to figure 1, Repeat the black, gold, purple, rose, aqua, and brown lines to create 48 diamond-shaped openings on the netting top (made of Bs and Cs). The actual count will vary according to bangle size. The bangles shown have 48 diamond-shaped units on the top—even numbers of openings are the easiest to embellish. Multiples of four are particularly suited to alternating embellishments. If you do not plan to embellish, the number of units is more flexible.

Stitch between the blue dot beads of the last round and the yellow dot beads in the initial loop, adding two Cs at a time on the top half of the netting tube and one A at a time on the bottom half. Weave in excess thread or reserve it for embellishment.

EMBELLISHMENT

Add various embellishments to the bangle tops to differentiate one from the other.

Work with a single needle and thread, and always reinforce every round for durability and structural integrity. Add most embellishments by stitching through the Cs in the top, outermost area of the netted bangle base indicated with yellow dots; add one embellishment style to the Bs indicated with blue dots. To begin the next embellishment, weave the needle through existing beadwork and thread paths to exit through the drop next to the yellow dot C.

Many embellishment variations are possible. Make extra tall bumps, incorporate 8° round seed beads, incorporate Czech fire-polished beads or crystals—the possibilities are unlimited. See figure 2.

Fig. 5

Stupa

Red line: Add two drops and two Ds alternately, stitching through yellow dot Cs. Blue line: Add four As by stitching through the drops and Ds added with the red line. Green line: Add four Cs by stitching through the As added with the blue line. Black line: Add four Ds by stitching through the Cs added with the green line. See figure 3.

Red line: Stitch through the Ds last added, pulling them into a little plus sign. Blue line: Add one drop to the top of the Ds last added. See figure 4.

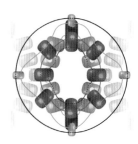

Fig. 6

Short Bump

Red line: Add four Es by stitching through the yellow dot Cs. Blue line: Stitch through the Es only, pulling them into a little plus sign. See figure 5.

Tall Bump

Red line: Add four Es by stitching through the yellow dot Cs. Blue line: Add four Es by stitching through the Es added with the red line. Green line: Add four 15°s by stitching through the Es added with the green line. Black line: Stitch through the 15°s only, pulling them into a little plus sign. See figure 6.

Chaton Montée

Red line: Add two 15°s by stitching through the yellow dot Cs and the blue dot Bs. Blue line: Add one chaton montée by stitching through the yellow dot Cs. See figure 7.

Bump with Rose Montée

Red line: Add four 15°s by stitching through the yellow dot Bs. Blue line: Add four Es by stitching through the 15°s added with the red line. Green line: Stitch through the Es only, pulling them into a little plus sign. Black line: Add one rose montée by stitching through the Es. See figure 8.

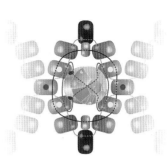

Fig. 7

Fig. 8

Bangle 1

Embellish every other opening with a stupa.

Bangle 2

Stitch a short bump to the first opening, skip an opening, stitch a tall bump to the next opening, skip an opening, and then begin the sequence again.

Bangle 3

Embellish all top openings alternately with rose montées and short bumps.

Bangle 4

Add a chaton montée to the first opening, skip an opening, add a short bump with As to the next opening, skip an opening, and then begin the sequence again.

Bangle 5

This is the flashiest pattern. Embellish all the top openings alternately with chaton montées and a bump with a rose montée.

Fig. 9

CHICLETS BRACELET

SUPPLIES

Beadweaving kit

Size 11° round seed beads:
  A, chartreuse matte, 15 grams
  B, matte gold, 6 grams
  C, permanent silver, 6 grams
  D, fuchsia matte, 2 grams
  E, aqua matte, 2 grams
  F, red-lined topaz, 2 grams

2mm sterling silver round beads, 530

12ss crystal AB rose montées, 80

16ss crystal AB chaton montées, 75

4mm 20-gauge closed jump rings, 6

4mm 20-gauge open jump rings, 12

32mm five-strand sliding tube clasp

Gold bead thread

Flush cutters

Chain-nose pliers

TECHNIQUES

Cuboids

Tubular one-drop even-count peyote

Building tubular peyote from right angle weave

Embellishing right angle weave

Closed jump rings to right angle weave

Modify multistrand clasp

Open jump rings

FINISHED LENGTH

8 ¾ inches (22 cm)

The name was adopted when my husband remarked that the finished bracelet reminded him of Chiclets gum. The bead colors are based on Swarovski's Kingfisher colorway.

OVERVIEW

Three lengths of simple beads rotate and swing around a peyote core stopped by right angle weave cuboids and are finished with multistrand components and a sliding clasp. Sterling silver beads and crystal montées in two styles add sparkle. Make the rotating beads, then the cuboids. Link the cuboids while incorporating the beads. Finish with the sliding multistrand clasp.

Note: The steps of creating this project are broken down into finite sections for the purpose of presentation; however, the method of organization may not represent how you prefer to work. For example, the core of tubular peyote lengths and right angle weave running the length of the bracelet may be completed in one continuous piece of beadwork. Also, spinning beads may be added at the end. There are numerous variations. I recommend beginning with the separate steps as they are written and assembling them in your own fashion.

SPINNING BEADS

Make two styles of spinning beads with 11°s in right angle weave and embellish them with chaton and rose montées and 2mm silver beads. Work with a single thread. Reinforce all beadwork with a second pass. Spinning beads are strung on the tubular peyote tube that joins two cuboids.

Five-Sided Bead in Two-Drop Right Angle Weave

Make this style of spinning beads with seed beads and 5mm chaton montées for embellishment. Make a total of five five-sided beads.

FIGURE 1

Work a length of two-drop right angle weave with eight Ds in each unit and four units long. Close the length into a tube when adding the fifth unit.

Fig. 1

FIGURE 2

Stitch one 5mm chaton montée to each right angle weave opening.

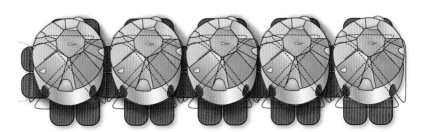

Fig. 2

FIGURE 3

Add one D between the two "up" beads of the right angle weave base. Add five Ds to each opening of the spinning bead.

Repeat to make four more in D. Repeat to make five each in E and F.

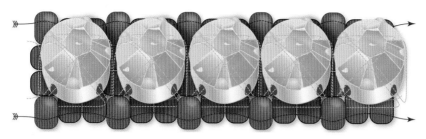

Fig. 3

Eight-Sided Bead One-Drop Right Angle Weave

Make this style of spinning bead with seed beads, 2mm rose montées, and silver seed beads. Make a total of 17 eight-sided beads.

FIGURE 4

Work a length of one-drop right angle weave with four beads in each unit and seven units long. Close the length into a tube when adding the eighth unit.

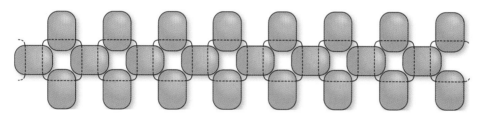

Fig. 4

FIGURE 5

Alternately stitch in one 12ss rose montée and one 2mm round silver bead to each right angle weave opening.

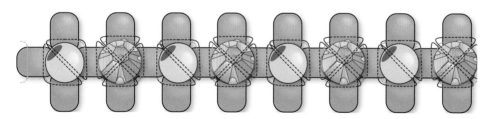

Fig. 5

FIGURE 6

Add one C between the single "up" beads of the right angle weave base. Add a total of eight beads to each opening of the spinning bead.

Fig. 6

CUBOIDS

Made of As and Bs in right angle weave, the two bases are then stitched together with 2mm round silver beads around four sides. Use a single thread throughout. Reinforce each right angle weave unit before adding subsequent units. Weave the thread ends in or save them for adding connections.

Note: From this point forward, placement of various color dot pairs is relevant to conserving space within bead holes. For example, where two bases are stitched together is a poor location to begin a connection, as the holes will become full of thread passes.

FIGURE 7

Work a base of A and B with B only at the center unit. Make a second, identical base.

FIGURE 8

Secure the beads indicated by red dots together in a circular stitch path; repeat with the beads indicated by blue dots. Bind the edges with a total of 12 2mm round silver beads.

Repeat to make 31 cuboids. Weave in all threads and set aside.

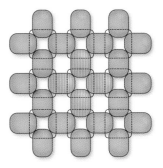

Fig. 7

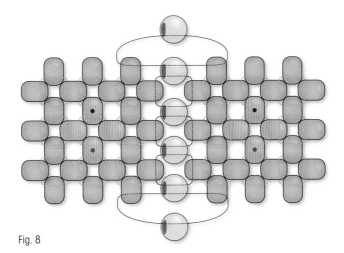

Fig. 8

CONNECTING

With B in tubular even-count peyote, stitch up from one cuboid to connect it to the next. Add one spinning bead before closing the connection. Add five-sided and eight-sided spinning beads alternately.

FIGURE 9

Exit from a base bead with a green dot. The first row of connection beads in tubular even-count peyote stitch will sit on top of a base bead with a red dot.

FIGURE 10

String one B and pass through the other base bead with a green dot. String one B and pass through the first base bead with a green dot. Repeat the thread path

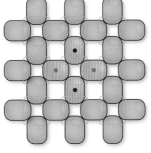

Fig. 9

Fig. 10

as though adding the new beads for the first time—this reinforces the row. Stitch through the first B just added.

FIGURE 11

String one B and pass through the next B from the previous row. Repeat. Reinforce. Step up through the first B just added.

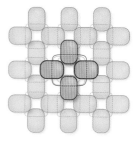

Fig. 11

FIGURE 12

Repeat figure 11 to add a total of seven rows. Slide a spinning bead onto the connection and exit the thread from one bead added in the last row with a red dot. Continue in tubular peyote and secure the beads with red dots to the next cuboid by alternately stitching through the beads with blue dots. The transition from connection to cuboid will appear seamless.

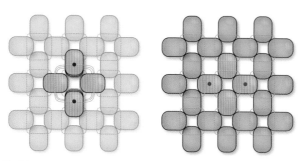

Fig. 12

MULTISTRAND END

Make two multistrand ends in much the same manner as the cuboids. Stitch in soldered jump rings and embellish with 12ss rose montées.

FIGURE 13

Work two bases in right angle weave 11 units long and three units wide with mostly A and some B. Secure the red dot beads of the first base to the blue dot beads of the second base—this is similar to figure 8, except this time you are stitching a red dot bead of the first base to a corresponding blue dot bead of the second base. Bind the edges by adding 28 2mm round silver beads in right angle weave. Embellish the green dot units with single 12ss rose montées as in figure 5.

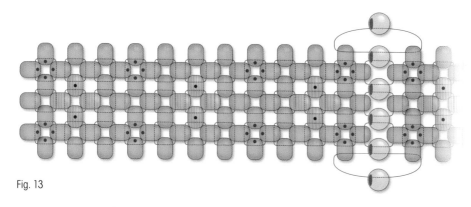

Fig. 13

FIGURE 14

Stitch closed jump rings to the same side of the multistrand end embellished with rose montées. Attach a jump ring to two opposing Bs of the same unit. Stitch in a figure eight through the Bs and the jump ring, and reinforce.

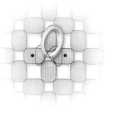

Fig. 14

FINISHING

Even all of the strand lengths by adding rows of tubular even-count peyote as needed. Take care that the overall length of each strand is approximately 1 inch (2.5 cm) short of the final desired length. Then, connect the final row to the base of the multistrand end as in figure 12.

With the flat side of a flush cutter against the clasp tube, remove the second and fourth loops—effectively making the five-strand clasp into a three-strand clasp with more space between each loop. Use two chain-nose pliers to connect the soldered jump rings stitched to the multistrand end to the three remaining loops on the sliding clasp. Add two jump rings to each clasp loop for a total of six open jump rings at each end.

If you prefer not to use open and soldered jump rings, add several more rows of peyote to both ends of all the strands, and then stitch the three remaining clasp loops directly to the multistrand end (the red dot units in figure 13).

CITY BEADS BRACELET

In the mornings when I taught for the Chicago bead store City Beads, the Chicago Botanic Garden was a short half-mile walk to the entrance from the hotel. As I walked across the Skokie Highway, the pattern in a cast-iron manhole cover repeatedly caught my attention, and it eventually became the inspiration for this bracelet. The rectangle shapes in relief inspired the placement of the large and small cuboids.

OVERVIEW

Make components and connect them with short tubular peyote to make the bracelet length. Add a bezeled rivoli for an accent in place of one cuboid. Finish the ends with closed and open jump rings, and add a modified multistrand clasp.

COMPONENTS

Make each component with a single thread. Adding silver bead embellishments causes the components to curve down slightly. Make 18 cuboids and 20 closed right angle weave tubes.

Large

This is a cuboid with exception for the width. Make it five units long and two units wide—this varies from the three-unit-wide cuboid directions in "Fundamentals." Embellish the length down the middle with four silver beads. Reinforce the embellishment with a second pass.

Fig. 1

Small

Stitch a three-by-three unit of one-drop right angle weave. See figure 2.

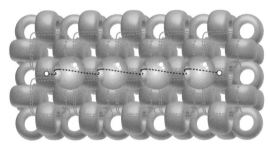

Fig. 2

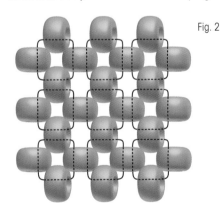

Fig. 3

Continue in right angle weave, adding four As (red dots) to close the tube length (red line). Cinch the four As at each end (blue lines). See figure 3.

SUPPLIES

Beadweaving kit

Size 11° round seed beads:
A, purple-lined transparent green rainbow, 16 grams
B, bronze metallic, 4 grams

Size 15° round seed beads:
C, purple-lined transparent green rainbow, <1 gram
D, bronze metallic, <1 gram

2mm sterling silver round beads, 72

12mm crystal vitrail medium rivoli

4mm round open 20-gauge jump rings, 12

4mm round closed 20-gauge jump rings, 6

41mm five-strand clasp

Flush wire cutters

Chain-nose pliers, 2 pairs

TECHNIQUES

Cuboids

Tubular one-drop even-count peyote

Building tubular peyote from right angle weave

Embellishing right angle weave

Right angle weave bezel

Closed jump rings

Open jump rings

Multistrand clasp augmentation

FINISHED LENGTH

7 ½ inches (19.05 cm)

Embellish the length with three silver beads. Reinforce with a second pass.

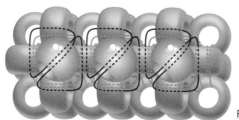

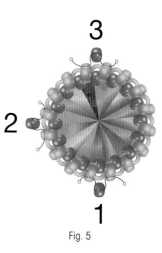

Fig. 5

Fig. 4

BEZELED RIVOLI

Use Cs and Ds to bezel the rivoli, then add connection points. This will ultimately connect two components and a peyote connection. See figure 5.

Use Cs for the 15×2 unit strip and to close the tube with a 16th unit. Use Ds to cinch the openings. Add Ds at three positions by stitching through the Cs. Reinforce the Ds.

CONNECTING

Components coalesce into a bracelet with three rounds of tubular peyote at each connection point. All connections are three rounds of one-drop tubular peyote. Seven large components in the bracelet's interior connect to small components at four points. Eleven large components on the left and right edges connect to small components at three points. Six interior small components connect to large components at four points. Fourteen small components on the bracelet edges connect to large components at three points. See figure 6.

ROW 1

Stitch a closed jump ring to the bottom edge of a small component (red line). *Stitch a three-round connection off the middlemost unit of the right edge (blue line), stitch a three-round connection from the top edge (green line), and stitch the last two beads of the connection just added to the middlemost unit of a large component (black line). Stitch a three-round connection from off the right edge of the large component (gold line). See figure 7 for thread path (gold line) to add the first round of two Bs by stitching through six As on the right edge of the large component. Stitch a three-round connection from off the middlemost unit of the top edge (purple line). Stitch the last two connection beads to the end of a small component (rose line).

Repeat from * to desired length, finishing with a small component. Stitch a closed jump ring to the last small component (turquoise line).

Fig. 7

ROW 2

Build up a three-round connection to the middlemost unit on the first edge (bottom) of a large component (red line). Stitch a closed jump ring to the last two beads of the connection just added (blue line). *Incorporate the connection from row 1 to the left edge of the large component (green line) using the thread path from figure 7. Stitch a three-round connection from off the right edge (black line) using the thread path from figure 7. Stitch a three-round connection from off the middlemost unit on the top

ROW 1   ROW 2   ROW 3

Fig. 6

edge (gold line) and stitch the last two connection beads to a small component on the bottom edge (purple line). Incorporate the connection from row 1 to the middlemost unit on the small component left edge (rose line). Stitch a three-round connection to the right edge (turquoise line) and a three-round connection to the top edge (brown line). Stitch the last two connection beads to the middlemost bottom edge of a large component (lime line).

Repeat from * to desired length, finishing with a three-round connection built up from the top edge of a large component (gold line). Stitch a closed jump ring to the last two beads of the connection (fuchsia line).

ROW 3

Stitch a closed jump ring to the bottom edge of a small component (red line). Incorporate the connection from row 2 to the middlemost unit on the left edge of the small component (blue line). Incorporate the D at the crystal bezel position 1 to the top edge of a small component (green line). Incorporate the D at position 2 to the connection from row 2 (black line). Incorporate the D at position 3 to the bottom edge of a small component (gold line). *Incorporate the connection from row 2 to the middlemost unit on the left edge of the small component (purple line). Stitch a three-round connection to the top edge of the small component (rose line). Stitch the last two connection beads to the middlemost unit of the bottom edge of a large component (turquoise line). Incorporate the connection from row 2 to the As on the left edge of the large component (brown line). Stitch a three-round connection to the middlemost unit on the large component top edge (lime line). Stitch the last two connection beads to the bottom edge of a new small component (fuchsia line).

Repeat from * to the desired length, finishing with a small component. Stitch a closed jump ring to the top edge of the small component (yellow line).

CLASP

Make a five-strand slide tube clasp into one that accommodates three strands by cutting off the second and fourth rings on each end. Use two jump rings to attach each soldered jump ring to one end of the clasp. Repeat to attach the second clasp end.

KARIN CUFF

Named for the person who crash-tested the first directions, Karin Salomon, this project came to me while walking along the Pacific Ocean on West Cliff Drive and listening to Ayn Rand's *Atlas Shrugged*.

OVERVIEW

Make a bunch of simple components. Connect them together in a magical manner with tubular peyote, and wrap it all up with a slick customized clasp.

CUBOIDS

Make 15 large cuboids and six small ones using A. Bind the first edge with alternating crystals and 2mm silver beads, and the remaining edges with A.

Large

Make 15 cuboids 11 units long and three units wide. Bind the front edge with an alternating pattern of 3mm crystals and 2mm silver metal beads (six each). Bind the remaining edges with A.

Fig. 1

Small

Make six cuboids seven units long and three units wide. Bind the front edge with an alternating pattern of 3mm crystals and 2mm silver metal beads (four each). Bind the remaining edges with A.

Fig. 2

FINISHING

Refer to figure 5 for the configuration for the large and small cuboids as well as the peyote tubes and findings. Components may be attached as they are created or attached once all components are complete—it is up to you. Due to the height from which the bracelet sits up off the wrist, an 8-inch (20.3 cm) bracelet fits a 6½-inch

Beadweaving kit

Size 11° round seed beads:
  A, opaque red AB, 43 grams
  B, matte translucent fuchsia, 15 grams

2mm sterling silver round beads, 114

3mm bicone crystal 2XAB beads, 114

4mm sterling silver jump lock jump rings, 20

4mm sterling silver soldered jump rings, 10

41mm sterling silver seven-strand sliding tube clasp

Red bead thread

Chain-nose pliers, 2 pair

Flush wire cutter

TECHNIQUES

Cuboids

Tubular one-drop even-count peyote

Building tubular peyote from right angle weave

Attaching tubular peyote to right angle weave

Closed jump rings

Open jump rings

FINISHED LENGTH

8 inches (20.3 cm)

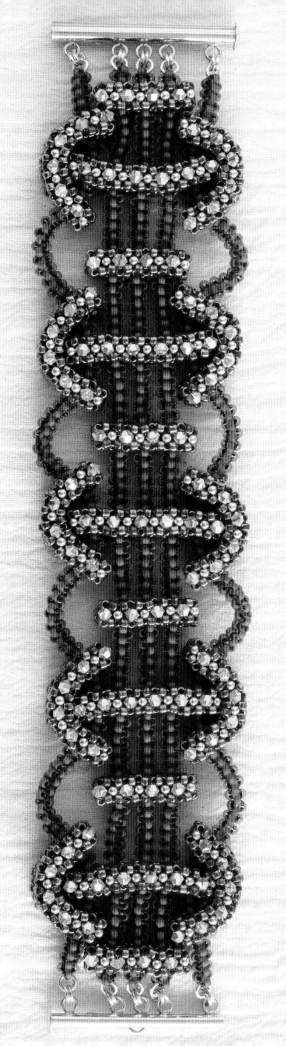

(16.5 cm) wrist nicely. Extend the length by adding a few more rows to the cuboids at the end or by adding one more small cuboid to each end.

There are units of right angle weave on both the left and the right faces of a cuboid where peyote tubes will be connected. Orange, yellow, green, blue, and purple sets of beads depict the five positions on a large cuboid.

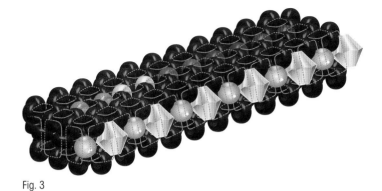

Fig. 3

Orange, yellow, and green sets of beads depict three positions where peyote tubes will connect to the small cuboid.

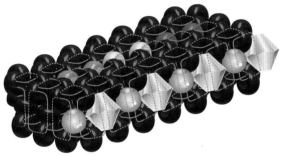

Fig. 4

Increase and decrease the number of peyote tube rows to adjust the length of the bracelet for a custom fit.

all large and small cuboids running down the bracelet middle are attached to six peyote tubes—three on each side.

19-row peyote tubes connect the outer purple position of one large, curved cuboid to the outer orange position of the next large, curved cuboid.

11-row peyote tubes connect large cuboids at the yellow, green, and blue positions to small cuboids at the orange, yellow, and green positions.

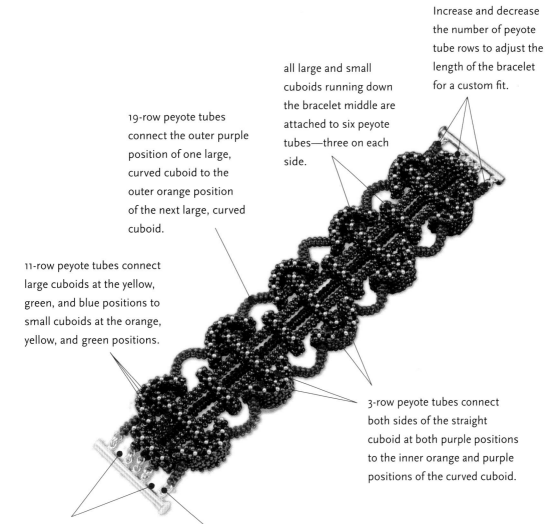

3-row peyote tubes connect both sides of the straight cuboid at both purple positions to the inner orange and purple positions of the curved cuboid.

Cut the second and sixth clasp rings with a flush cutter. Cut the corresponding rings from the second end of the clasp for the other end of the bracelet.

Stitch in one soldered jump ring to the end of all 10 peyote tubes. Then, attach the soldered jump ring to the clasp with two jump rings each.

Fig. 5

NACHO LIBRE BRACELET

SUPPLIES

Beadweaving kit

Size 8° bronze
metallic round
seed beads,
<1 gram

Size 11° round seed
beads:
A, opaque
turquoise, 7
grams
B, bronze metallic,
4 grams
C, opaque red AB,
7 grams

Size 15° round seed
beads:
D, bright gold
metallic,
2 grams
E, bronze metallic,
<1 gram

Red bead thread

TECHNIQUES

Right angle weave

Tubular peyote

Right angle weave
ring

Peyote bead

FINISHED
LENGTH

7 ¾ inches (22 cm)

Named for the thematic colors of my favorite Jack Black movie, this piece is made of right angle weave components linked together with tubular peyote. The component shape recalls the dramatic lucha libre mask eyeholes.

OVERVIEW

Make right angle weave components and link them together with short lengths of tubular peyote. Finish with an asymmetric loop and bead clasp.

COMPONENTS

Make the drop-shaped components by joining two faces of 11° and 15° beads worked in right angle weave—five each of A and C.

In right angle weave, stitch a face of As and Ds. See figure 1. Stitch a second face.

Line up the faces and bind the outer edge with 19 As. See figure 2. Bind the inner edge with seven As and 10 Ds. Join the components with peyote lengths originating from the binding beads indicated with blue and green dots.

Repeat to make a total of five components each of As with Ds and Cs with Ds.

Fig. 1

Fig. 2

CLOSURE AND JOINS

Tubular peyote stitch lengths join all components in an offset pattern. Add a right angle weave ring and one peyote bead to each end. Join all components with bronze Bs worked in tubular peyote. Long joins are nine rounds long, and short joins are three rounds long. See figure 3.

Make two right angle weave rings 12 units around with 15°, 11°, and 8° Bs and Es. Set these aside.

Connect the turquoise components in sequence at the blue dot beads (figure 2) with five long joins. Stitch a long join to the last component and build a peyote bead with As starting with the eighth and ninth rows. Stitch a short join to the last A component and stitch the third row to a right angle weave ring.

Repeat to join the C components, stitch on a right angle weave ring to the first component in the same manner, stitch a long join to the last component, and build a peyote bead with Cs in the same manner. Connect the A and C components with 11 short joins at the green dot beads (figure 2).

Fig. 3

POP BEAD BRACELET

This fun, sparkly bracelet is like delicious, salty potato chips—you need more than one!

OVERVIEW

Make a handful of components with a peyote bead on the first end and a right angle weave ring on the second end.

COMPONENTS AND FINISHING

Stitch a right angle weave ring 12 units long and close it with a 13th unit. Set it aside. Make a peyote bead, beginning with a four-bead loop. Stitch 10 rounds of tubular peyote to the cinch row of the peyote bead. Continue in tubular peyote stitch to incorporate the beads in the final tubular peyote round to two 3mm crystals. Repeat to make 12 more components or as many as needed. Pop a peyote bead of one component through the right angle weave ring of the next component. Repeat to create a length of components.

SUPPLIES

Beadweaving kit

Size 11° opaque red AB round seed beads, 8 grams

Size 15° round black opaque seed beads, 3 grams

3mm jet 2XAB bicone crystals, 130

Black thread

TECHNIQUES

Peyote bead

Tubular peyote

Right angle weave ring

FINISHED LENGTH

8 inches (20.3 cm)

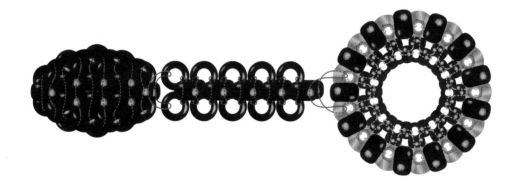

Index

Note: Page numbers in *italics* indicate projects.

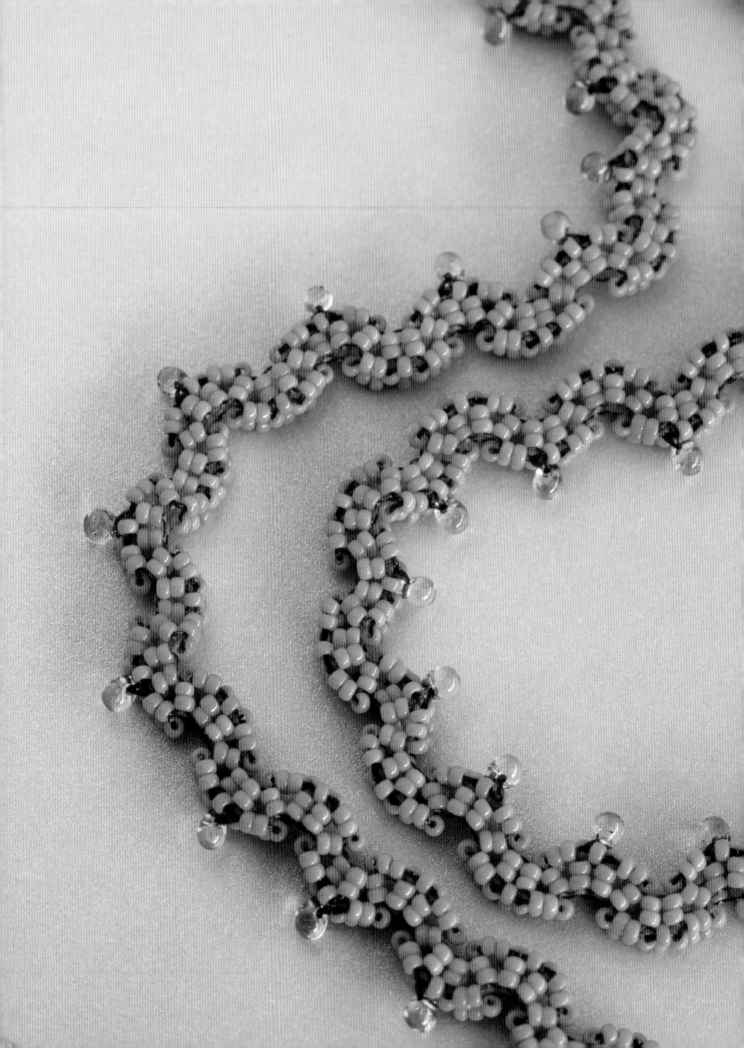

About the Author

Rachel Nelson-Smith is a master beadweaver. She lives in Santa Cruz, California, with her genius husband and fearless toddler. This is Rachel's third book. Examples of her vibrant work have appeared in numerous publications, museums, and galleries. Since 1996, she has taught jewelry-making and has spoken on the process across the United States and internationally. In fall 2015, she will study art at UCSC.

Visit her website, www.rachelnelsonsmith.com, where you'll find her schedule and photos of her beadwork.

Acknowledgments

Colin Smith persevered through this project and our first two years of parenting. He diligently provided support when work hours and motivation needed boosting. Ray Hemachandra first breathed life into the project, and I'm thankful for his belief in my work. His vision of beading projects on par with those offered at national bead shows was his genius stroke, as I've been off the teaching circuit while caring for my first child. Special thanks goes to Nathalie Mornu, Kevin Kopp, Jill Jarnow, Kimberly Broderick, Karen Levy, Lori Paximadis, Lorie Pagnozzi, and Marilyn Kretzer for their successive ministrations, and Diana Ventimiglia for bringing it home. Heartfelt thanks go to Barb Switzer for technical editing and to Lynne Harty for fine photographs. Thanks to Robert Fenwick, I wrote down and reached the goal of writing three books.

31901056917950